PEOPLE'S CHRISTIANITY

People's Christianity

Theological Sense and Sociological Significance

THEOLOGY AT THE FRONTIERS SERIES

Jose Mario Francisco, SJ,
and Jayeel Cornelio

Paulist Press
New York / Mahwah, NJ

Cover image by DavidZydd/iStock.com
Cover design by Dawn Massa, Lightly Salted Graphics
Book design by Lynn Else

Library of Congress Cataloging-in-Publication Data
Names: Francisco, Jose Mario C., author. | Cornelio, Jayeel Serrano, author.
Title: People's Christianity : theological sense and sociological significance / Jose Mario Francisco, SJ, and Jayeel Cornelio.
Description: New York / Mahwah : Paulist Press, [2022] | Series: Theology at the frontiers | Includes index. | Summary: "This book calls for a deeper appreciation of people's religious lives, through which they encounter God and relate with other people"—Provided by publisher.
Identifiers: LCCN 2022012644 (print) | LCCN 2022012645 (ebook) | ISBN 9780809155545 (paperback) | ISBN 9781587689512 (ebook)
Subjects: LCSH: Christian life.
Classification: LCC BV4501.3 .F7352535 2022 (print) | LCC BV4501.3 (ebook) | DDC 248.4—dc23/eng/20220624
LC record available at https://lccn.loc.gov/2022012644
LC ebook record available at https://lccn.loc.gov/2022012645

ISBN 978-0-8091-5554-5 (paperback)
ISBN 978-1-58768-951-2 (e-book)

Published by Paulist Press
997 Macarthur Boulevard
Mahwah, New Jersey 07430
www.paulistpress.com

Printed and bound in the
United States of America

Dedicated to the faithful in the margins

Contents

About the Book

People's Christianity: Theological Sense and Sociological Significance approaches lived religion through the eyes of faith and the interdisciplinary lenses of theology and the social sciences. "Sense" and "significance" encapsulate the book's two main goals. First, it unpacks how people's Christianity manifests the laity's faith and how it thus becomes a *locus theologicus* that reveals new reflective horizons. These reflections cover a wide range of themes from pastoral to critical. Second, it points to lived Christianity's significance, properly understood in relation to its social context or realities. Resisting the theological and moral condescension toward popular expressions of the Christian faith, this book argues that they are, in fact, meaningful if assessed in light of the daily realities that confront local believers. Foregrounding experiences in the Global South, the book will speak to Christians from different traditions and theological perspectives. Ultimately, it calls for a deeper appreciation of people's religious lives, through which they encounter God and relate with other people.

Preface

Many would not dispute the sense and significance of how Christians live faith in their various contexts. However, the basis for their faith as well as how they shape religious practice need elaboration. This is a book of pastoral and practical theology that seeks to understand how Christians live their faith on several fronts.

Between the social sciences and theology. We have each been trained in one of these disciplines, but with profound interest in and familiarity with the other. Though cognizant of their historical boundaries and theoretical issues, we have chosen not to begin with a methodological discussion. Instead, we start by carrying on a conversation for a mutual enrichment and wider understanding of lived Christianity.

Between lived Christianity in the Global South and in the North. This book is written from a decidedly Southern perspective from which it employs many examples. Furthermore, the dynamics of lived Christianity represented in these examples have analogies found in other contexts.

Between Catholic and other Christian traditions. Though many source materials come from Catholic tradition, other Christian traditions speak of similar concerns using different vocabularies. A common thread that runs through the book is the desire of ordinary people—the laity—to encounter God in meaningful ways.

We hope our book will be of interest to Christians from different traditions and varied perspectives. In reading it, may they discover fresh ways of appreciating their religious lives, encountering God, and relating with other people.

Acknowledgments

Writing this book has taken us many years to finish, a process that involved many working lunches at the Jesuit Residence at the Ateneo de Manila University. Both of us would like to acknowledge the contributions of our colleagues throughout this process. Jose Mario acknowledges the valuable contribution of the academic communities at Boston College (USA), the Pontifical Gregorian University (Rome, Italy), and the Loyola School of Theology, Ateneo de Manila University (Manila, Philippines). Discussions with students and colleagues at these institutions helped generate critical questions and insights addressed in this book. Jayeel is grateful to the Divinity School of Chung Chi College at the Chinese University of Hong Kong (CUHK), which hosted him as a visiting professor in 2018. In that capacity, he developed a course on pastoral sociology, whose ideas became the basis for some of the chapters in this book. Jayeel acknowledges the fruitful intellectual engagements with colleagues and students at CUHK.

We are deeply indebted to Fr. Mark-David Janus at Paulist Press for proposing and nurturing the series Theology at the Frontiers. The editorial board of the series chaired by Gerard Whelan of the Pontifical Gregorian University and our colleagues at Paulist Press, especially Melene Kubat, who facilitated the production of this book. Paul McMahon, the Editorial Director, took time to work through our manuscript. We appreciate him for his attention to detail and for making sure that our book is featured in the Theology at the Frontiers series.

Finally, we thank Robbin Dagle for his editorial assistance in the preparation of the final manuscript. Funding support for this project partially came from the Ethnographies of Philippine Auditory Popular Cultures (EPAPC) project, which received a grant from the Commission on Higher Education (CHED) and the National Commission for Culture and the Arts (NCCA) in the Republic of the Philippines.

PART I

SMELLING THE SHEEP

1

The Authenticity of the Popular

FOR SOME CHRISTIANS, it is idolatrous; for others, it is mindless fanaticism. The privileged think of it as hooliganism. In their view, its devotees—many of whom are urban poor—are undisciplined, leaving behind a trail of rubbish in the wake of the procession. Commentators have labeled it as "*batya't palu-palo* spirituality," invoking Filipino terms for washbasin and wooden club that urban poor women use when doing their laundry by hand.[1]

Whatever outsiders say, there is no denying that the Black Nazarene continues to attract an increasing number of followers. Every year, millions of devotees flock to the district of Quiapo in the city of Manila to participate in the *traslacion*. On January 9 every year, the *traslacion*—a Spanish term for "passage"—reenacts the transfer of the image of the suffering Christ that took place in 1787 from its original site in an Augustinian church in Intramuros, Manila, to the basilica where it is now venerated.[2] Lasting hours, the procession traverses the narrow streets and bridges of the capital city to its destination. Slowing down the procession are the Black Nazarene's barefooted devotees, the majority of whom are men. They clamor to reach the carriage to wipe the image with their towels, which is then given, they believe, divine healing power that can then be brought to a loved one in need of healing.

What makes the image popular is the compelling belief in its miraculous attributes. While many are there to seek healing or an answer to their deepest prayers, others are committed devotees, returning in gratitude after experiencing a miracle in the past. These narratives account for the enduring attraction of the *traslacion* and the many other yearlong practices surrounding the Black Nazarene.

The story of Virginia Cantos, who is now in her seventies, is typical. Three decades ago, she turned to the Black Nazarene when the doctor, who was to operate on her tongue cancer, failed to show up. She took it as a sign. For nine Fridays, she committed to attending masses in the basilica. Free from cancer since, Virginia remains a devotee of the Black Nazarene to this day.[3]

The Black Nazarene is just one of the many images that attract a massive following in the Philippines. The country, which is predominantly Catholic, has many devotional practices dedicated to the Virgin Mary, the Child Jesus, and saints who have an answer to every problem. While the laity might take these practices for granted, the richness of these devotional practices in the Philippines and elsewhere challenges scholars, observers, and religious leaders regarding what they mean for the Christian today. Apart from the condescension that these practices elicit from outsiders, other questions are far more important: Why are they pervasive? Why do they endure? And what do they mean?

While there is no one answer to these questions, this book provides some insights and hermeneutical tools through our sociological and theological backgrounds. Our proposition is that lived religion—or what we call people's Christianity—embodies *theological sense* and *social significance*. This introductory chapter explains what we mean by people's Christianity by attending to the scholarship on lived religion and addressing the loaded concept of authenticity.

Smelling the Sheep

To comprehend people's faith in the Black Nazarene, Filipino theologian Mark Calano proposes, first, understanding the interplay between the *poón* (the image of Christ) and *panata* (devotion).[4] Devotees are in an intimate relationship with the *poón*, which is mediated by the white towels but is also embodied in their choice to be barefooted during the procession. Being barefooted expresses the desire to be close to the very suffering of Christ. Rejecting the condescension of outsiders, Calano asserts that "if we listen to devotees…we get an inkling that *panata* is a response to the faithfulness, love, and special grace that the *poón* has given to them. There is a sense of specificity and privacy at work here that necessitates the promise to renew their commitment annually by attending and participating in the *traslacion*."[5]

For sociologists, the power of a religious moment lies not only in the stories about it but also in the solidarity that people find in it. At one level, its devotees find solidarity with the very image of Christ. The Black Nazarene is the God who suffers. It is black, the color of death. It carries the cross, the symbol of the burdens of life. It is exposed to the elements, which speaks of human vulnerabilities. At the same time, people find solidarity with one another, even if they may be in competition with one another for the attention of the suffering Christ. The *traslacion* is, after all, the kind of devotion not meant for the faint-hearted. They are all there as devotees. They are all there seeking a miracle. They all have an unwritten affinity with one another by virtue of their shared experiences of illness and defeat. In other words, their solidarity with the suffering Christ is also solidarity with one another. The procession affords them what sociologists call collective effervescence, a sensation of belongingness.[6] Only those who are part of the ritual will understand it. What is chaotic to the outsider is, in fact, full of order to the insider.

But recognizing this internal order does not mean that the entire procession is heaven on earth. A closer look reveals problematic contradictions. The first is that it all takes place in Manila, a city described as the "gates of hell" in Dan Brown's *Inferno*.[7] The issue, of course, is not whether the streets of Manila are supposed to be secular and therefore spared from any religious event, but, rather, that alongside a compelling religious moment there exist corruption and poverty. This is what makes the public display of the religious devotion to the Black Nazarene a far more meaningful and disconcerting moment at once.[8] These contradictions manifest themselves in the ills of urban decay: homelessness, informal settlements, the underground economy, and even the proliferation of illegal drugs.

The other issue concerns the devotees' desire for healing and the inadequacies of the health-care system. Although strides have been made, health care remains expensive and prohibitive in the Philippines. The rich and some middle-class Filipinos can enjoy private health care, but the same cannot be said of the wider population. Thus, at its core, the devotion to the Black Nazarene is a desire for better things. *Ginhawa*—a Filipino term for relief from pain, suffering, difficulty, and any need—is a desire that, while elusive to many, nevertheless remains an aspiration.[9] Consequently, the procession is an assertion of the people's right to the city and its offerings of the good life. It is, therefore, a religious devotion as much as it is also a public protest.

This opening vignette demonstrates the richness of popular religion once it is approached through the eyes of faith and the interdisciplinary lenses of theology and the social sciences. This process is the endeavor of *People's Christianity*. Theological sense and social significance encapsulate our two main goals. The first is to unpack how people's Christianity—popular religion—manifests the laity's faith and becomes a *locus theologicus* that reveals new reflective horizons. These reflections cover a wide range of themes from pastoral to critical. The second is the significance of popular religion that can be properly understood in relation to its social context or realities.[10] Resisting the theological and moral condescension toward popular expressions of the Christian faith, we argue that they are in fact meaningful if assessed in light of the daily realities confronted by local believers. From the point of view of sociology, popular religion embodies social realities that matter to the everyday experiences of believers. Therefore, gender, class, culture, geography, and history are some of the important aspects that allow for a more comprehensive view of popular religion.

To recognize the sense and significance of people's Christianity is our attempt at heeding Pope Francis's call for pastors around the world to "be shepherds, with the 'smell of the sheep.'"[11] In the foreword for Pope Francis's book, Bishop Robert Barron suggests that the idiom is a pastoral call not only for ministers to be available for those in need. Proximity to the sheep is a criticism of careerism and worldliness that Pope Francis has observed among the clerical ranks. Barron also suggests that the joy of the minister is to be found in the calling and purposes of God.

What Is People's Christianity?

There are, of course, many ways of smelling the sheep. This book situates it in the specific context of popular religion or what we refer to as *people's Christianity*. As already noted, theological sense and social significance imbue popular expressions of people's faith, even if some may readily dismiss them. In our view, doing so aligns with the reflexive writings by such scholars as Lamin Sanneh to locate Christianity in various settings around the world.[12] For him, world Christianity "is the movement of Christianity as it takes form and shape in societies that previously were not Christian, societies that had no bureaucratic tradition with which to domesticate the gospel. In these societies, Christianity was received and expressed through the cultures, customs, and traditions of the people affected."[13] As a concept, world Christianity pays attention to local adaptations of the faith—people's Christianity. These local adaptations are most evident in popular expressions of the faith, whose theological underpinning is the incarnation. As Bhakiaraj notes, "If in the Christian foundational belief of Incarnation, God came to dwell among humans, then the same Divine expresses itself in particular human categories of language and culture."[14]

In the latter part of the twentieth century, scholars paid attention to popular religion primarily as an attempt to move away from the longstanding debates on religious decline in the West. Thus, in the past three decades, the literature has established a thematic consensus on what constitutes popular, lived, or everyday religion. For Ammerman, who has reviewed the extensive scholarship since the 1990s, lived religion is often defined by what it is not: laity and not the clergy; practices and not beliefs; practices external to religious institutions and not internal; and emphasis on agency and not on collectivities.[15] Although the study of popular religion is now dominated by sociologists and anthropologists, the field emerged when historians in the 1990s came together to interrogate the history of religion through the experience of ordinary people.[16] In fact, the very term *popular religion* was itself popular among historians who were interested in how Reformation theology was received and appropriated by believers. These historical writings readily observed the tension between institutional religion and its "unauthorized" counterpart. In effect, these historians "underscored the politics of religious practice: on the one hand a politics of regulation from the center, often with some measures of success; on the other an extraordinary array of practices arising out of custom, improvisation, and resistance."[17]

The tension between official and everyday religion continues to be an important analytical matter for observers, even if many have already veered away from the debate. Certainly, there is some merit in asserting the distinction between institutional and popular religion. This distinction reveals the analytical appreciation for different ways of being religious. It is particularly helpful in making sense of the gap between taught religion and practice in everyday life, a point that perhaps matters far more for religious institutions that value "right" norms and beliefs in the process of religious socialization.[18] The distinction also matters in contemporary conversations about spirituality. Both scholars and practitioners frame spirituality as a deinstitutionalized mode of approaching the sacred.[19] In this light, the identifier "spiritual, but not religious" is both an everyday and a theoretical concept in the social sciences.[20] In both senses, contemporary spirituality is about the ongoing seeking ethos, which is often private or only internal as a rejection of institutional affiliation or boundaries.[21]

Despite the conceptual distinction, the line between institutional and lived religion is often artificial.[22] This is especially the case for individuals and communities who draw on the practices of institutional religion in their everyday contexts. Rituals, festivals, and processions are activities in which the distinction is blurred given that, as many of the examples in this book will show, a symbiotic relationship exists between clergy and the laity. Recognizing this relationship thus avoids pitting people's Christianity, as lived religion, against institutional Christianity, a tension that is ironically the default assumption in many studies of popular religion. This new recognition is not only true for the social sciences that pay attention to the replication of the sacred in everyday life,[23] it is even at the heart of many theological reflections about the piety of ordinary believers—a recurring theme in this book. Indeed, long-held scholarly assumptions about religion, such as eternal truths and supernatural reward, are not always of prime importance for people. It is in this light that "religiosities—plural—is...the right word, wherever one is observing."[24]

The distinction between institutional religion and lived religion is not always clear-cut. Historically oriented writings about spirituality assert this point. Although spirituality is often associated with religious activities that are hybrid and deinstitutionalized, its origins point to a different scenario. The emergence of spirituality in the Anglophone world in the nineteenth century began as an attempt to reform churches until the relationship could no longer be sustained.[25] Sociologically, it is also possible for people to describe themselves as "spiritual, but not religious" to refer to the ways they navigate religious institutions. In

Cornelio's study, Filipino Catholic youths who are otherwise involved in outreach activities or communicating with God in their own ways refer to themselves in this manner to account for their nonparticipation in Mass.[26] They believe that through their participation in alternative activities or prayer forms, they are more authentic to their Catholic identity than those who are more traditionally pious and yet unfair in their dealings with other people. Cornelio builds on the concept of reflexive spirituality to demonstrate how young people make sense of their faith theologically and practically so that it becomes consistent with what they believe is the essence of being Catholic. As a concept, reflexive spirituality has also been useful in understanding how ordinary Christians grapple with disagreements they have with official doctrine proclaimed in their congregations' pulpits without leaving them.[27]

In this book, we wish to move beyond the debate between institutional religion and lived religion. In fact, it does not help to begin with this assumption. We agree with Mary Jo Neitz, who points out that to study lived religion is "to understand the various ways that people now are using religious/spiritual practices in their daily lives to connect to traditions."[28] We also agree with anthropologist Peter Bräunlein's ethnographic conclusion based on his work among participants in Holy Week crucifixions in the Philippines: "Filipino individuals who are nailed to crosses and repeatedly confirm 'we are 100% Catholic' are challenging our own basic assumptions. To take them seriously means to examine our analytical instruments seriously and carefully."[29]

Thus, instead of reverting to the tension between institutional religion and lived experiences, we focus instead on the *theological sense* and the *social significance* that underpin people's Christianity. This is a meaningful endeavor at two levels. At one level, our approach recognizes the different ways in which ordinary people have appropriated Christianity to relate to their conditions. Thus, Christianity becomes far more meaningful and embraced by local communities. At another level, people's Christianity is also a *locus theologicus*. Local practices embody beliefs and convictions about the Divine and their sense of faith about how God operates in the here and now.

By paying attention to Christianity as lived religion in this manner, our work aligns with recent developments in the study of religion. In her influential work, Meredith McGuire argues that when scholars pay attention to "religion-as-lived," they discover that "religion—rather than being a single entity—is made up of diverse, complex, and ever-changing mixtures of beliefs and practices, as well as relationships, experiences, and commitments."[30] A person's ability to connect them in the context of everyday life is what establishes ownership. At the same time, her project challenges conventional scholarly assumptions about religion as a coherent whole that is transmitted from one generation to another. Instead, she recognizes that religion is an ever-evolving set of beliefs and practices that is more hybrid than is often accepted by outsiders.

Our work also aligns with recent developments in the study of Catholicism (and Christianity at large) in the Global South. A native of Cameroon, Jesuit anthropologist Ludovic Lado proposes that "to be a Catholic in Africa as anywhere else means different things to different people both in terms of personal trajectories and religious expectations."[31] In other words, for ordinary Christians, their religious identity is multilayered; theology, culture, politics, and history all come together in devotion. The only way to access these layers is by recognizing that this devotion exemplifies people's Christianity, a faith that is received, appropriated, and owned in the context of lived experiences. Elsewhere in this book we refer to this as the practical rationality of people's Christianity.

Thus, the result is that people's Christianity must be read in the plural: *people's Christianities*. The diversity within Christianity, therefore, is exemplified not only by theological reflections grounded in local realities. Rituals, practices, and other religious activities reveal the rich tapestry of world Christianity.[32] Although it has the tendency to elicit negative remarks, lived religion deserves serious consideration—if only to smell the sheep and be embedded in the complex realities confronting Christians around the world. Many lessons are derived from this insight for sociological thinking, theological reflection, and even pastoral work in places where dissent is often silenced.[33]

Authenticity

The recognition of religious authenticity lies at the heart of our approach to people's Christianity as lived religion. Concerning religious authenticity, two questions often arise for scholars, pastoral workers, and religious individuals: Is it authentic to official doctrine and liturgy? How do we interpret and understand hybrid religious practices among ordinary people? In our view, however, these questions only rearticulate the tension between institutional religion and lived religion, one that needs to be abandoned. In effect, we cannot assume that "religious affiliation or membership is somehow a master category that determines an entire set of norms for an individual member's entire faith and practice—allowing some practices as 'good' or consistent with the organization's religion and condemning others as 'bad' or even heretical."[34]

THE SOCIOLOGY OF RELIGION

In the sociology of religion, the concept of authenticity echoes the broader literature. Focusing on the history of the West, Charles Taylor recounts the progress of the subjectivist turn in contemporary culture to account for the search for what feels real for many people.[35] In this culture, the introspection of the self becomes the mechanism to understand one's identity and assess one's choices and actions. The sociology of religion echoes this theme in terms of religious individualization. Underlying this trend is the process of detraditionalization in which external sources of authority are taken over by an internal one—the self.[36] Many cases exemplify this, chief of which, as we have noted, is the rise of alternative spiritualities in the West.

Another emerging area of investigation related to individualization is prayer. In recent years, the sociology of religion has become interested in the prayer lives of people. In Western contexts in which institutional religious affiliations and practices have declined, prayer has been noticeably robust in mundane experience. This is an example of the endurance of religion in people's lived experiences, a point that Italian sociologist Giuseppe Giordan makes. Based on his qualitative research among Italian young adults, he proposes that their prayer life has taken on postmaterialistic themes, focusing, for example, on well-being and satisfaction instead of money.[37] A theological shift has also taken place along these lines. The usual attention to sin and the "fear of eternal damnation" have given way to the pursuit of "higher and higher levels of personal well-being—even the relation with the sacred is interpreted in such framework, as an instrument useful to discovering the 'true self.'"[38]

Recognizing the authenticity in lived religion calls into question taken-for-granted concepts in religious studies. At the turn of the century, historians, sociologists, and anthropologists began problematizing claims that local beliefs and practices are split-level, "cafeteria," or selective, and therefore are not fully developed.[39] In reality, the convictions and practices of ordinary Christians, even if they may not be endorsed by their denomination or congregation, are very much tied to their Christian identity. For example, drawing on his work among American Catholics, Baggett presents that there are many who now believe that one can be a "good Catholic" without necessarily following the church's teachings on abortion, marriage, or even the resurrection of Christ.[40] In fact, it is possible that these "nonaligned" convictions are far more common than religious leaders are willing to admit. Indeed, in Baggett's own research, even those who detest cafeteria Catholicism are, when probed, selective when it comes to certain doctrines or liturgical practices. Among Protestants, the same dynamic is at play, especially for those who are considered "Golden Rule Christians."[41] These individuals, many of whom are liberal in orientation, are bound together not by doctrinal allegiances but by the philosophy that they must be good and caring toward other people in their respective spheres of influence, including the family, the neighborhood, and the workplace. Heavy concepts such as salvation are downplayed. For conservative Christians, the theological convictions of Golden Rule Christians can no longer be taken seriously. But Ammerman asserts that, from the point of view of lived religion, the latter's communal life is how they apply their Christian faith and relate to God.

Authenticity might come across as a virtue for highly individualized societies. But scholars are also beginning to recognize that it is not any less pronounced for the rest of the world, with implications for how lived religion must also be understood. The work of Peter Bräunlein on passion rituals in the Philippines is instructive. He rejects specifically the dichotomy between authentic and inauthentic because it simply replicates the stereotype that the West is rational while the developing world is highly religious.[42] By abandoning these distinctions, observers can then appreciate the authenticity that underlies religious practices, including flagellations and human crucifixions during Holy Week. In fact, based on his extensive ethnographic work, he realizes that for those who participate in these tortuous and spectacular rituals, "we are 100% Catholic."[43] For the flagellants, their physical sacrifices bring them to a much closer intimate relationship with the God who is also suffering with and for them. This is a significant view from the inside that outsiders often miss when they consider only either the pain or its fanaticism.[44] The insight here is that the view from the inside reveals the very process of localization or translation.[45]

Thus, from the point of view of the social sciences, authenticity is both a virtue and an analytical concept insofar as religion is concerned. As a personal virtue, authenticity emphasizes people's search to be real, aligning their lived religion with how they understand who they are deep inside. As a social scientific concept, authenticity recognizes people's religious actions to be meaningful not only to themselves but also in relation to their everyday realities, issues, and concerns.[46] Consequently, authenticity is not to be confused with sincerity, whose interior orientation is analytically inaccessible to the observer. What is accessible to the observer are the religious practices and the narratives by which these practices are recounted and explained.

THE THEOLOGY OF AUTHENTICITY

The theme of authenticity is also discernible in theological thought insofar as the latter relates to local conditions and the collective actions they inspire. Arguably, the theme of authenticity is the implicit assumption in contextual theology, as Christians around the world, especially in the Global South, have "realized that the Gospel must become contextual by addressing the concrete problems of the context."[47] One is reminded of the Dalits in South Asia, the Minjung in South Korea, and the peasants of Southeast Asia, all of whom have developed very concrete theological views about Christ, the Scriptures, and the empowering work of the Holy Spirit in the here and now.

Cultural engagement is one key area for authenticity in contextual theology. In the experience of many Christians in Asia, the cultural diversity on the continent has become a resource instead of competition for the gospel. The belief in the Incarnation, for example, is alive for Asian Christians, who can imagine Christ in a different light—as the Sage for the Chinese and the Adi Purusha (primordial man) for the Indians. Similarly, the Holy Spirit is understood through the lens of energies as Asian Christians draw on their personal experiences with *pranah* (breath) and *Qi* (energy), ideas that give "the Spirit also an ecological dimension."[48] These illustrations point to the ability of theological reflections among ordinary people to localize Christian beliefs in the context of their own social and cultural experiences. To this end, interreligious dialogue is essential to contest the pessimism of some churches or denominations toward other religions on the continent. Many Christians have done pioneering work in this area. Some of them have become influential theologians themselves. In India, Vandana, for example, has established an ashram where Catholics and Hindus can come together to do meditation and practice the triple yoga of *jnana* (knowledge), *bhakti* (devotion), and *karma* (action). For practitioners, meditation aims to "awaken oneself to the identity between oneself (*atman*) and God (*Brahman*), in the way Jesus came to realize his oneness with the Father at the River Jordan."[49]

To be authentic, however, can also be a transgressive assertion as far as broader norms are concerned. Theologians have been reflecting on this point as well in recent years. While there are many theological sources that we explain elsewhere in this book, a point of entry is pastoral theology. "The study of lived religion," argues Susan Dunlap, "encourages pastoral theologians to see individuals and communities as creators of culture in a theological idiom."[50] But she presents this in a countercultural fashion. "If scripture and theology have been established as essential and primary sources for pastoral theology, and if the theories of power which reveal the destructive operations of white supremacy, patriarchy, and other power formations have also been established as intrinsic to excellence in pastoral theological scholarship, then the study of lived religion further highlights the generative, constructive dynamics of local communities."[51] The key point here is that from the believers' vantage point, the transgressive character of lived religion reinforces its authenticity for ordinary people. In a way, the illustrations above concerning the cultural engagement of the gospel are transgressive, especially when contrasted with colonial forms of Christianity. They can be contrasted with fundamentalism too, which renders other religious practices as evil. But the theological transgressiveness of lived religion lies as well in its emancipatory motivation and ambition. Indeed, when borne out of the sufferings people face daily, these theological reflections are organic.

The emergence of Black liberation theology in South Africa testifies to this point. Confronted with the realities of apartheid, genocide, and dispossession, ordinary Christians and activists produced their own theological reflections about Jesus as the "fighting God" incensed by corruption and exploitation.[52] Its message brought Christians together in the struggle for justice but also gave them joy in that their collective work was cast in truth and freedom. The main premise of Black theology, as inspired by the activist Steven Biko in the twentieth century, is the "singularity of Blackness as a *condition* of oppression, exploitation and subjugation, which, when the oppression is properly understood and oppressed people rise up to claim their dignity and freedom, is turned into a condition of resistance."[53] The authenticity of the message lies in what it was critiquing: a theology of whiteness, brought by European missionaries, to equate subservience to them with obedience to God.

The transgressive character of organic (contextual) theology is evident too in the experience of the queer community. This much is true especially in LGBTQ+-affirming congregations. In Nairobi, Van Klinken's extensive ethnographic work reveals the power of ordinary queer Christians to come together to contest homophobia.[54] In Kenya, the state and many Christian churches reject queer identities and communities. Despite this rejection, five young people, believing in the God of inclusion, came together to establish Cosmopolitan Affirming Church (CAC). Located in downtown Nairobi, CAC holds fellowships, Bible studies, and discussions of faith and sexuality in anticipation of "'the city yet to come,' a city with freedom not only for the expression of religion but also for diverse sexualities."[55] Even the congregation's choice of name is transgressive for its members. "Cosmopolitan" asserts that they are together despite their many differences.

The final example sheds light on recent developments within Evangelicalism. Although Evangelicalism began with a progressive ethos in the nineteenth century, it became more associated with conservative politics on hot-button issues such as abortion and same-sex marriage.[56] In many parts of the world, the face of Evangelicalism is the megachurch, known for its spectacle and middle-class aspirations.[57] But in their own ways, young Evangelicals around the world are embracing their progressive origins, a trend that could also be explained by demographic shifts and attitudinal changes among the youth. In New Zealand, Christian millennials are participating in social justice training, which includes immersive trips around Southeast Asia.[58] These Christian youths have a strong global outlook and are convinced that the gospel has to be rendered visible through social justice. This is a significant theological shift. They are clearly disillusioned with what they deem as the apathy of their respective congregations.[59] Rivera's work demonstrates how the character of lived religion is transformed for Evangelicals as they are immersed in a global community of like-minded individuals and exposed to the injustices in many parts of the world. In their own ways, they are transgressing and reforming the theological boundaries of Evangelicalism to make their Christianity porous to the needs of the world.

These theological developments reveal the relational aspect of authenticity that is clearly embedded in communities of faith. But these relations are also embedded in unequal power relations in society. In lived Christianity, it becomes evident that authenticity is made manifest by how ordinary people build these relationships with one another and ultimately with God. Consequently, the quest for authenticity is a process toward greater authenticity and not an unchanging state of existence. From this perspective, authenticity in lived Christianity is an ongoing practice more than it is a once-and-for-all possession.

Flow of the Book

Probing the sense and significance of people's Christianity is our way of smelling the sheep. In other words, people's Christianity is evident in how ordinary Christians live their religion in the context of their everyday situations. That is where one finds social and theological depth, an important lesson for people of faith. As we have recounted above, these situations are often replete with injustice, inequality, and disorder. At a closer look, people's prayer lives, religious rituals, and other spiritual activities reveal much of the conditions in which they are embedded. Therefore, lived religion embodies social significance.

But ours is not a validation of materialist views of religion that render its beliefs and practices as opium of the people. As we have noted, transgressiveness permeates people's Christianity and is often directed at the prevailing order that excludes the most vulnerable in society. It may also be directed at the prevailing order within the church, especially schemes and practices that fail to recognize the other within its ranks. Recognizing this transgressiveness is often a difficult feat, as it tends to be countercultural and even counterintuitive for those used to fundamentalist or theological lenses that exclude certain sectors. And yet, as this introduction has carefully laid out, it is in people's Christianity where rich theological insights emerge.

Maintaining an interdisciplinary approach, we will explore people's Christianity. The book is divided into three parts. The first part, which includes this chapter, introduces the argument of the book. The second chapter presents the diversity of lived Christianity around the world. But instead of simply giving a comprehensive overview of different forms of lived religion, it traces the four sociological elements of people's Christianity: authenticity, the location of the sacred, the presence and mediation of sacred power, and practical rationality as the basis of people's Christianity. The concept of authenticity, which has been mentioned in this introduction, will be revisited alongside these other three elements. Collectively, they point to the immanence of lived religion.

The second part is about "Reading between the Lines," in which we present two perspectives of lived Christianity. The first views lived Christianity as a form of worship. Chapter 3 thus offers a close reading of the *Directory on Popular Piety and the Liturgy: Principles and Guidelines*. An official Vatican document, the *Directory* acknowledges the spiritual value of popular piety in which the gospel takes on forms that are tangible and relatable to ordinary people. The chapter ends with an honest assessment of the *Directory*'s claims, especially highlighting its inadequacies. Reading between the lines of the *Directory*, we pay attention to its failure to consider the link between popular piety and the totality of Christian life. Chapter 4 maintains the critical perspective by turning to the emancipatory themes discernible in popular religion. It begins with an overview of general liberation theology and the theology of the people. The chapter ends by reflecting on the divergence between the *Directory*'s attempt to align popular piety with official liturgy and the liberationist perspective to link popular religion with people's daily struggles.

The third part is about "Sensing the People's Faith," in which theological reflections are necessarily informed by an ethnographic viewpoint that acknowledges human agency in popular religion. Although dependent on divine revelation, human agency is evident in the very process of reception or localization. Such theological reflections go beyond the themes of worship and liberation presented in the second part of the book. Specifically, people's Christianity has an integral aspiration that brings together the totality of human experience. We assert this point in chapter 5, in which lived Christianity is read in the light of Christian tradition. Its main argument is that lived Christianity has a place in Christian tradition, which finds its basis in God's self-disclosure and inclusive character. In this view, the people of God are not passive recipients of divine revelation. They are subjects, whose active work lies in appropriating this tradition in living Christianity and passing it on to other people. Thus, we can say that lived religion, which is inseparable from the totality of human experience, is a *locus theologicus*. Chapter 6 illustrates this point by focusing on Marian devotions. Once again, localization as a process resurfaces here in making sense of the diversity of Marian practices around the world. Throughout the colonial period, images of Mary were brought to the colonies, where they took on local identities that reflected the livelihood of people, flora and fauna, and folklore. But it is also in this process of localization that divine revelation can be contextually understood. The theological insight here is that Marian devotions around the world reflect the work of the Holy Spirit in communicating God's self-disclosure to the faithful in and through the human and historical character of these contexts. Finally, in chapter 7, we spell out the theological value of human agency in the *sensus fidei*. From an institutional perspective, the *sensus fidei* assumes an approbative mode of reception, a collective process that evaluates the alignment between reception and revelation. But this chapter pursues a more pastoral approach in regarding these practices and how Christians live their faith in their everyday life and contexts. One can begin adopting a pastoral approach by engaging in active listening to the people of God, no matter how imperfect they might be. The chapter ends with a bold declaration: Sensing the faith from below and at the periphery provides the hermeneutical key to the faith of God's people and Christ's disciples and to the approbative reception of specific religious practices.

The two chapters in the final part, "Journeying with the Sheep," present the new analytical and pastoral horizons. In chapter 8, we revisit the complicated and yet fascinating relationship between theology and sociology, the two disciplines within our analysis of lived religion that tend to be suspicious of one another. And yet bringing them together is analytically fruitful throughout this book. In a manner that heeds the call to "smelling the sheep," we argue in chapter 8 that its practical applications are just beginning to emerge in the areas of *sensus fidei*, *pastoral sociology*, and *public theology*. Finally, in chapter 9, we reflect on Pope Francis's call to journey together. As *synodos*, the church must move toward greater authenticity in the faith, drawing even closer to the way of Jesus.

Conclusion

"Smelling the sheep" is an apt idiom to describe our approach to appreciating people's Christianity. Our working assumption is that authenticity imbues the lived religion of ordinary Christians. We have indicated how this view distances the book from conventional assessments that pit lived religion against institutional religion. While that might still be analytically useful, our work attends instead to the sociological and theological underpinnings of people's Christianity. These underpinnings are fundamental to our question, "What meanings are conveyed in people's lived religion?"

The themes within this book—worship, liberation, agency in tradition, and the ability of the faithful to discern the things of God—echo our fundamental premise about the authenticity of popular religion. Expressed differently, lived Christianity embodies the attempts of ordinary Christians to relate to the divine and with other people. But lived Christianity is also about God's dealings with people in the here and now. This relationship is thus dynamic, which calls for the interdisciplinary dialogue that this book initiates between theology and the social sciences. Indeed, the following theological reflections recognize the role of cultural diversity in this relationship between God and humanity. But at the same time, the authenticity of lived Christianity lies in being transgressive. It is countercultural especially in ways that challenge structural violence in society and even in one's religious community. And as we have explained, the transgressiveness of people's Christianity is a result of a long discernment process especially among the powerless.

But our work is not only an academic exercise. The reflections also have implications for public discourse about lived religion and on pastoral ministry. At its core, "smelling the sheep" is not an academic exercise. It is about being embedded in the everyday realities of the people of God, many of whom are distant from the center of power.[60] For Pope Francis, this is about pastoral proximity and pastoral availability for those who are in the peripheries. His call has a concrete expectation that the clergy will be present in the lives of the marginalized. The caveat is that spiritual detachment from prestige, comfort, and power are all elements that are paradoxically very present in the everyday life of pastors. In the context of our work, our humble proposition is that lived religion is an entry point for ministers and the wider pastoral community to recognize the lived conditions of ordinary people. In their lived religion, their deepest aspirations are very much present, informing their very beliefs and practices and the ways they relate to the divine and with one another. To be present in people's Christianity is a practical implication of our work making the listening tools of pastoral theology and social research valuable.

But to be present with ordinary people calls too for participating in their own struggles. Indeed, in many circles, people's Christianity is an act of resistance. We have indicated the rich theological developments among the marginalized, especially in places imbued with strife and inequality. We also know that alternative theological insights are emerging among youths who are disillusioned with their respective congregations' inability to confront global injustices. It is by recognizing lived religion's transgressiveness that our approach does not abandon the possibility of critique. To appreciate people's Christianity is thus not to romanticize lived religion. In recent years, scholars of lived religion have begun to entertain the question whether critiquing lived religion is possible without being reductionist. Anthropologist Kim Knibbe asks, for example, "How can we think about the possibility of engaging in a critique of religious practices, structures, and lifeworlds that we study while not retrenching to a reductionist, flattened, and objectifying mode of considering (religious) lifeworlds, reducing them to a form of 'false consciousness'?"[61] Based on her ethnography, the answer lies in probing the ways in which lived religion reinforces power asymmetries, structural violence, and inequalities in society.

We trust that this book will inspire reflections beyond the intellectual exercise that it is. By appreciating people's Christianity as the locus in which the active work of God meets the agency of ordinary individuals and communities, our work is a contribution to the advancement of the Christian tradition. Nothing can assert the authenticity of the popular in a far more convincing manner than the dynamism of this relationship.

2

The Diversity of Lived Christianity

VATICAN II RECOGNIZES the role and contributions of the laity in enriching the church as the people of God.[1] For this reason, Marian piety, devotion to saints, and even the activities of basic ecclesial communities are celebrated for embodying the spirituality of the laity. But not all forms of everyday Christianity are celebrated. Some also face resistance, especially from religious leaders. This is not surprising. Christianity, as it is lived and experienced by ordinary believers, is not often coherent to an outsider. Nor can it be expected to align fully with patterns and practices prescribed by the hierarchy or religious experts.

Religious leaders then call on the faithful to temper their practices, which they often characterize as excessive, superstitious, or immature. The influence of some forms of Buddhist and Hindu meditation in the prayer life of Catholics, for example, has been associated with demonic and New Age practices.[2] In this light, the *Directory on Popular Piety and the Liturgy* spells out principles, so that "pious exercises" conform to the "doctrine, legal discipline and norms of the Church."[3] The resistance, however, is not only theological. Cultural differences, because of migration, for example, can also spark liturgical tensions that were previously not present. African Catholic immigrant communities in the United States, for example, are known for their expressive singing, ecstatic dancing, and colorful dresses. While their ways point to the life and vibrancy of new parishes, local Catholics might find their growing presence a threat. At a recent Catholic conference in the United States, a participant suggested that "these Africans are taking over our churches. They want their celebrations to go on forever, and it affects the other activities of the community."[4]

Our approach here is to view people's Christianity in terms of the religious lives of ordinary individuals. The ones who attract our attention are neither experts nor professionals within the religious hierarchy. We are essentially more interested in the sheep than in the shepherds. Although official doctrines and practices are still important, our curiosity lies in how they are received and appropriated by ordinary individuals.[5] These appropriations manifest themselves in the practice, experience, and expression of religion "by ordinary people (rather than official spokespersons) in the contexts of their everyday lives."[6] For these individuals, conventional distinctions between sacred and profane, official and nonofficial, correct and incorrect, and religious and nonreligious do not necessarily matter. This is because their religious expressions are embodied, communal, and underpinned by rationalities that make sense to them as religious actors. Our approach, therefore, is not juridical toward people's practices regarding correct or acceptable religious behaviors. The everyday life is the site in which we can understand the sense and significance of an influential religion such as Christianity.

In other words, people's Christianity lies in "what people do with religious idioms, how they use them, what they make of themselves and their worlds with them, and how, in turn, men, women, and children are fundamentally shaped by the worlds they are making as they make these worlds."[7] From this vantage point, everyday religion is, at its core, the religion of ordinary people. It might be arbitrary or excessive to an outsider but sensible to the practitioner.

Lived religion, however, is not an individualistic phenomenon. Much of popular religion is a shared experience with like-minded folks. Individuals undergo formal and informal socialization shaping their beliefs and practices. These everyday beliefs and practices also have implications for interpersonal relationships. Prayer, for example, while an interior moment of connecting with God, is deeply implicated in the life of the community. The prayer life of young people, as Mason's study among participants in the World Youth Day in Sydney shows, is associated with higher religious practices such as Mass attendance and confession.[8] Prayerful youth are also more involved in volunteering and giving to charity. In other words, people's lived experiences of Christianity show that religion remains a communal matter. They are the sheep whose lives exemplify the diversity and communal vibrancy of people's Christianity in the world today.

As we noted in the previous chapter, much of the judgment against popular religion is misplaced and is derived from unfamiliarity with the filtering mechanisms of people's reception. Therefore, we give attention to the sense and significance of Christianity for different people. Indeed, the long and rich history of religions around the world shows that beliefs and practices are never revealed as a complete set from their origins. While the growth of Christianity stems from a received tradition and a "chain of memory" that affirms communal belonging, it is also beholden to local meanings.[9] This explains why converting locals, which was among the chief goals during the colonial period, was not an easy feat for missionaries. It was not so much about language barriers as it was the untranslatability of certain Christian ideas such as soul, sin, and repentance, for example, that colored their reception.[10] Individuals had to understand and, at the same time, enact on their own what they had received from missionaries. Along similar lines, liturgy, despite representing approved structures of prayer by the church, must also factor in local experiences of the faith. Liturgical inculturation, if it were to be successful in local contexts around the world, needs to listen to people's "often unarticulated but nevertheless deeply held religious sensibilities," which are often expressed in popular piety.[11]

Lived Christianity is a moment of reception as much as it is an ongoing negotiation with what people receive from the institution and the many other religious sources that surround them. Reception, therefore, is not a passive episode in the life of a believer. It has a hermeneutic sense, which brings together simultaneous processes of understanding, interpretations, and application on the part of believers.[12] Reception also matters to the institution that prescribes beliefs and practices. True to the character of lived Christianity, these processes are not necessarily coherent and systematic. On some occasions, people's Christianity also demonstrates not just negotiations, but active modes of resistance that call for the reform of religious institutions in terms of their structures and beliefs.[13]

The theological enterprise, of course, interrogates the complex relationship between local reception and the approbative function of the whole church in the light of *sensus fidei*. But this enterprise is not the focus of this chapter; we will return to it in chapters 7 and 8. We are also aware that there is resistance to the contribution of sociological research to grasp the empirical realities of the faithful in the settlement of "doctrinal or moral issues in the life of the Church."[14] Instead, our intention, here, is to take stock of people's Christianity as it is experienced around the world.

Sociological Elements

The accounts in this chapter are not necessarily exhaustive. Nevertheless, they are indicative of the rich trends that characterize today's lived Christianity. We frame these trends in terms of the sociological elements of popular Christianity. In this chapter, we spell out four crucial considerations: the authenticity of people's Christianity; the location of the sacred; the presence and mediation of sacred power; and practical rationality as the basis of popular religion. These elements manifest the significance of Christianity to its followers around the world. In adopting a sociological approach, we hope to avoid exoticizing popular religion, which implicitly reinforces its perceived opposition to prescribed modes of Christianity. Specific examples will accompany each of these elements to showcase the sense and significance of people's Christianity.

AUTHENTICITY

Our starting point for making sense of people's Christianity is the assumption that for its practitioners, everyday religion is an authentic expression. Although some of these religious expressions may not necessarily be officially sanctioned, they are still authentic insofar as they reveal the longings and dispositions of practitioners. Consequently, the authenticity of everyday religion is as much about being true to the self as it is about being part of a religious community. As Bräunlein points out in his ethnographic work on Holy Week rituals in the Philippines, those who undergo self-flagellation and crucifixion assert that they are "100% Catholic."[15] Among outsiders, the perception is that these acts are inauthentic or premodern. It is premised on the view that a correct form of

Christianity exists, often in terms of restrained piety. The essentialism is also inflected with the assumption that only the West is modern. But none of these pious followers sees their acts as irreligious. For them, they operate in a relationship that commits them to God via miracles and their petitions. The relationship is not only transactional. It is also intimate, in which the flagellant shares with the suffering of Christ.

From this perspective, assessments that consider popular religion as an example of split-level Christianity fail to see the coherence of piety for individuals and communities. Split-level Christianity refers to the seeming contradictions among the religious practices of individuals who profess to the faith. The metaphor is derived from a two-story house in which the activities on one level contradict those that take place on the other.[16] Split-level Christianity thus assumes there is a coherent spirituality from which everyday religion deviates. The only problem, however, is that such coherence is institutionally defined by which practices are acceptable. Consequently, split-level Christianity, as a concept, is more doctrinally prescriptive than sociologically descriptive. Clearly, from the point of view of the flagellants described above, there is no apparent contradiction between their devotion and their Catholicity.

Observers are increasingly recognizing the authentic character of people's religious expressions. In the literature, this trend is described as the scholarly turn to everyday authenticity.[17] Many of these observers are sociologists and anthropologists who are discovering the complex ways in which people tackle faith issues and religious practices. Their assessments reject the dichotomy engendered by a juridical approach to popular religion. These assessments also recognize that boundaries among religious beliefs and practices are mostly synthetic. People draw from different religiosities and sources of inspiration that, in fact, deepen their connection with the divine. In fact, religious practices, even those claimed to be received traditions within Christianity, have the imprint of intercultural influences. Hybridity is the very nature of religious life, and it is perhaps more acute now given transnational flows. Consequently, there is a need to "grasp the complexity, diversity, and fluidity of real individuals' religion-as-practiced, in the context of their everyday lives."[18]

At the same time, theologians and religious leaders have become more reflexive about their own predispositions, especially in the context of missions and pastoral work. Liturgy with its prescribed rubrics, for example, carries public and personal meanings for its participants. For instance, Mark Francis recounts that, as a young priest in Colombia, parishioners reprimanded him for not kissing the feet during the ritual of the Washing of the Feet during Holy Week, even if it was in keeping with liturgical protocol.[19] While it was not in the rubrics, the parishioners complained that he did not follow the example of Pope John Paul II, who did exactly that. Reception, in other words, is a critical component of people's Christianity. Reception is the moment in which religion becomes meaningful to an ordinary believer.

However, to treat everyday authenticity in religious life as a largely individualistic effort is a mistake. Much of everyday religion is situated in communal relationships and wider social contexts. Many Christians feel the compulsion for their beliefs to speak to social and political issues. In other words, their sense of authenticity lies not simply in an individualistic religious expression. Surrounded by injustice and inequality, believers draw inspiration from theological reflections to offer an informed response. The response can be political for church communities that fight for the struggles of the poor, especially in contexts in which Christianity is a religion of the poor. Dionisio's work, for example, reflects on the need to transform churches so they become one with the poor.[20] In contexts of social injustice, the issues are diverse. In some communities, environmental concerns are matters of ecological and social justice around which basic ecclesial communities are organized.[21] In many places where gender discrimination still exists, Christians are also organizing themselves in ways that contest it not just in society but even in their own faith traditions. Dignity, for example, a national organization of gay and lesbian Catholics in the United States, has organized activities such as Pride Sunday in their local communities. In such events, they effectively change the character of the Catholic Mass through its music, liturgy, and symbols to be more welcoming of queer people. The symbolic act demonstrates their commitment to transforming not just society but the very religion with which they identify. It is through this activist religiosity that they maintain the authenticity of their sexual and religious identities.[22]

LOCATION OF THE SACRED

With 480,000 attending its services, Yoido Full Gospel Church is one of the world's largest Protestant congregations.[23] Like many other

Protestant churches in South Korea, its growth accompanied the stellar economic performance of the economy in the postwar period. It began as a congregation in a shantytown but moved and eventually settled on the island of Yoido. It has satellite churches throughout Seoul. Yoido's movement, however, is not only accidental; in effect, its movement followed the very expansion of Seoul into the megacity that it now is, transferring where new developments emerged. This expansion also mirrors the fortunes of other Protestant denominations that turned the once peripheral South Korea into a "spiritual center of global Christianity."[24]

But the spatial configurations of Yoido and many other Protestant denominations in Seoul are also indicative of the tensions between them. Their locations indicate class differences, owing much to their history and success over the decades. At the same time, their worship styles are indicative of their class placements. Yoido's services are very Pentecostal, the attendees of which express their worship through "yelling, chanting, and wailing."[25] Other denominations in Seoul take pride in their solemn approach, which, they argue, is what makes them attractive to intellectuals. Harkness's rich ethnographic accounts show that the marked differences between these congregations are reinforced not just by physical distance but also by embodied worship. Other Protestant denominations associate Yoido with shamanism, which, in their view, is of "the lower class and poverty, with the rural, folk, and superstitious, and with spiritual settings of earlier times."[26] Such discourses do not necessarily come from church leaders but from their own members.

The location of religion is, therefore, not a neutral matter. Space is imbued with meanings for religious individuals. Through space, we find not just the sacred but also markers that emphasize remarkable differences that assert identities, feats, and distinct theologies.[27] Space is thus very much implicated in the tension between popular and official religion.[28] It is also very much implicated in the religious experiences of individuals and communities. These implications need to be surfaced in understanding the location of the sacred for people's Christianity.

Focusing on geography primarily sheds light on how religious boundaries are, for the most part, porous for ordinary believers. Religious encounters with the divine can take place "at a mountain brook or the mountain-side hermitage of a twelfth-century holy man…in Ave Marias at the shrine of Our Lady of Lourdes or…the river that runs beside it."[29] The distinction between the sacred and the profane is not clearly defined in everyday religion. This shows that for people, Christianity is not necessarily a separate category of their existence. It is as mundane as much as it is transcendent. Ordinary sites can become sacred locations. In other words, at these sites, religious moments intersect with everyday concerns. The geographer Elizabeth Olson records, for example, that crosses are built on the peaks of the town of Hanocca in Peru.[30] Members of the community climb the mountain once a year to offer produce such as potatoes. Offerings are also made to Mother Earth to petition for a bountiful agricultural cycle. In contrast to Yauri, a neighboring *pueblo* associated with Evangelicals, Hanocca's crosses and ritual mark the district's very strong Catholic identity.

A spatial approach to understanding people's Christianity shows that even decidedly secular spaces can have a religious character. Most likely, the assumption that some spaces are devoid of religion is a product of the secularist project. The place of religion in the city, for example, is carefully managed by the state since its streets are supposed to be public spaces. And yet, everyday religion is very much present in such secular spaces in the form of processions, for example. Such spaces, however, can also become contested sites for religious groups. In this light, politics in the city are about "religious boundaries and processions."[31] Over the past decades, the annual procession of the Black Nazarene in Manila has been attracting millions of devotees. Although the demographics are now changing, many of these devotees are still male and come from a low-income background. Such composition is not accidental. The procession, which can last over twenty hours, demands brawn and commitment. In such an event, men compete for a spot close enough to the icon that they can throw a towel upon it or touch the long rope attached to its *andas*, or carriage. The belief is that the touch transmits miracles. This demographic composition is very telling. Apart from demonstrating masculine religiosity, the annual ritual, for taking over the streets, is also an assertion of the right to the city that has displaced the urban poor.[32]

Finally, while there is a tendency to see place as a unique and isolated moment, it is implicated in broader structures enhanced by globalization. New ways of thinking about the emplacement of everyday religion help us reflect upon "the mobility of ideas, of bodies, and of rituals and practices across space."[33] It is therefore not surprising to see common religious practices in the form of shared songs, theologies, rituals, and other forms of religious socialization around the world. What is being engendered by "religious globalization" is a "convergence and conformity of religious practice."[34] Facilitating this convergence is technology and heightened mobility of religious practitioners. In terms of the homogenization of practices, Kong's approach to religious globalization, for example, can be seen in her analysis of the Alpha program in Singapore. Alpha is an evangelistic program that originated in the United Kingdom, the design and curriculum of which is fully adopted by various Evangelical congregations and Catholic parishes in Singapore. It has attracted highly educated and cosmopolitan Singaporeans to consider Christianity as a relevant faith to which they could convert. Religious globalization, in this light, appears to be a process that diffuses from a center, with localization that minimally changes the form and substance of religious practice. But focusing on everyday religion might offer a different nuance. The globalization of Christian music, for example, whether through popular culture such as movies or religious bands, varies according to the "interpretive lens through which the global community filters the musical exchange."[35] It is not surprising, then, that English contemporary Christian music produced by megachurches in the West are common in Evangelical and Catholic youth circles around the world. They are appropriated in terms of local translations and musical styles and sung in light of people's everyday needs.

THE PRESENCE AND MEDIATION OF SACRED POWER

One of the main points about the location of the sacred is that boundaries between sacred and profane are typically porous in everyday religion. In other words, people's Christianity senses the presence and power of God even in mundane or secular spaces. By the same token, it also means that a place does not have to be historically important for it to imbibe a religious character. For everyday Christians, the porousness of space is thus also about the presence and mediation of sacred power. Sacred power is very much embedded in the sense and significance of Christianity to people.

Such is demonstrated by the emergence of alternative pilgrimage sites in popular Christianity. For example, pilgrimage sites are typically associated with a historically important event such as the birthplace of

Christ or a divine moment such as an apparition of Mary. But other religious sites can also become centers of pilgrimage, not for any historical or divine moment but for the healing experiences they offer. This has been the experience of Our Lady of Snows in Illinois. Attracting thousands of pilgrims every year, it has built even larger retreat facilities to accommodate visitors. This just shows that the validity of a religious experience is not contingent on whether a place has historical connections to a religious moment. In his assessment of religious pilgrimage and everyday life, Swatos is correct in suggesting that a site "becomes holy by virtue of what happens in the here-and-now and not because of any connection with a charismatic past."[36]

That sacred power operates in the here and now is a significant character of people's Christianity. In this light, popular religion is less about the other world than it is about everyday concerns. And because much of these concerns have to do with suffering, popular religion is ultimately life affirming.[37] Thus, in people's Christianity, suffering in this world and faith in the divine are deeply intertwined in a way that once again troubles the distinction between sacred and profane. Sapitula's landmark work on devotional practices to Our Lady of Perpetual Help in Manila is instructive. Letters from 1948 to 2008 indicate gratitude and petitions to God and the Virgin Mary.[38] Personal issues revolved around well-being, employment, education, health, and business. One of these letters, written in 2005, illustrates how devotees related to Mary:

> After 10 years [of] working abroad we agreed to have a little business.... Mama Mary, we thanked you so much, after ten long years, we were able to save money to buy a house and car to use for our business.... I was very thankful that our lives with our little kids ran smoothly. We went into construction business. At first, it went good even without investing [much] capital.... We initially thought, this is it, we have the break [we need]....
>
> We tried a partnership with a big company to secure good contracts, hoping that would be the solution. But that was the start of everything that led us to where we are now.... IS IT WRONG TO ASPIRE FOR ADDITIONAL INCOME? We went bankrupt and had court cases filed against us by our suppliers, until we sunk in debt. We tried

> to start anew…but we fell all the more and until now we haven't recovered. I know that you sent all these tests to us. Everything is meant for a reason. And I accepted all of these [willingly].[39]

Essentially, sacred power, for everyday believers, can diffuse itself in everyday life. This attribute is another way of thinking about lived religion in general and people's Christianity in particular. Christianity can only make sense to people when the metaphysical aspects of the faith are rendered "visible and tangible, present to the senses in the circumstances of everyday life."[40] The power of people's Christianity lies in the intersection of everyday needs and the experience of the sacred.

One practical implication here is that for pastoral work to be truly effective, religious experience needs to intersect with everyday realities. The consistent and intimate practice of the body is crucial in making this happen. In his work on everyday religion, Orsi suggests, for example, that rituals and material aspects of religion such as images in and of themselves do not carry the power of the sacred. Sacred power, however, gets transmitted in the form of experience, which is why, in catechetical instruction, for example, participants are enjoined to meet images with devotional sincerity in the form of prayer and acts of love.

This intersection between interiority and materiality is what makes sacred power pervasive in people's Christianity. Rituals are effective where such dynamism is evident. Material religion is effective insofar as an individual approaches it with devotion. Consequently, the seeming contradiction between pilgrimage and tourism is resolved by devotees themselves. The act of contemporary pilgrimage may have encountered criticisms for they are often couched as tourist activities. But people's sense of the sacred may not necessarily make proper distinctions between consumption of religious experience, travel, and motivations underpinned by a desire for the divine to meet their needs.

No wonder, then, that prayers, when answered, are attributed to God as miraculous manifestations of his sacred power. The same can be said about petitions to specific saints or icons. Indeed, *National Geographic*'s rich accounts of Marian devotion around the world testify to how suffering enriches people's ways of approaching the Virgin Mary. Miracles, sightings, and mystical experiences all come together to render Mary the "world's most powerful woman."[41] Whether these encounters are officially recognized by the religious institution is immaterial.

The point is that the experiences are real for people and become pivotal moments in their lives. At the same time, suffering, instead of fostering doubt, creates an atmosphere to discover one's religiosity.

One story is about fifty-nine-year-old Arthur Boyle. Diagnosed with cancer and given only a few months to live, he came to Medjugorje in the hope of finding a miraculous intervention. The Virgin Mary did not fail him. After going to confession, he went to see a visionary called Vicka in a jewelry shop. Vicka prayed for him and right there and then he felt a sensation that caused him to sweat. When he returned to the United States, he went for another check-up, and the CT scan showed that his tumor had already shrunk. He now leads pilgrims to Medjugorje and acts as a "mouthpiece for Jesus Christ's healing power and of course the Mother and the power of her intercession."[42] Arthur's narrative demonstrates that popular religion is deeply embedded in their everyday needs. While sin and forgiveness are crucial aspects of Christian doctrine, it appears that miracles, as they are experienced by the body, are more potent in turning people's lives around. Such encounters with sacred power engender devotions that last a lifetime and can spill over to succeeding generations.[43]

PRACTICAL RATIONALITY

Some public commentaries against popular religion tend to frame it as irrational religiosity. For these commentaries, popular piety reeks of magic and superstition. It is thus neither intellectually sound nor scientifically justifiable. These judgments can also derive from a particular type of theological reflection about popular religion, one that resists what it considers religious excesses in the form of fanaticism. Religious experts, for example, debate every year whether the annual procession of the Black Nazarene in the Philippines is an expression of faith or fanaticism. While priests recognize the sincerity of people's devotion, other people may not be as sympathetic. In his now defunct and once influential blog, Marcos described devotees as "fanatics" who "believe that the statue can do miracles, heal the sick, gives [*sic*] good fortunes, etc."[44] The author viewed the devotion to the Black Nazarene as a form of fanaticism for its rowdiness, noise, and superstitious beliefs about the image itself. He even considered it an idolatrous act tolerated by the religious institution. This view conveniently overlooks the motives and aspirations of the people who participate in the devotion.

But we argue that these motives and aspirations are what underpin the rationality of people's Christianity. This is the final sociological element we wish to highlight in this chapter. Rationality—that which drives people's actions—is very practical in that it is primarily informed by experience. This point needs to be carefully explained. We deviate from the limited understanding of rationality as reasoning based on logical deliberation or empirical science. Instead, we draw inspiration from Max Weber, who suggests that the rationality of religion for people is not always a result of careful deliberation. Instead, it is underpinned by much socialization that keeps religion grounded.[45] Religious beliefs are, for one, falsified by experience. In the long run, those that do not resonate with people's experiences and expectations fade away. In other words, they no longer make sense in people's consciousness. But once verified by experience, religion becomes a very convincing fact of life. This explains why much of popular devotion is not so much about sin as it is about the experience of miraculous interventions—past, present, and future. Therefore, religion is a "chain of memory" not simply through institutional affiliation but more by how faith resonates from one generation to another.[46]

What makes popular religion practical is that it is consistent with human experience. On the one hand, it is consistent with the needs and aspirations of people. Indeed, the conventional view of popular religion is that the devotion of the masses is largely about their uncertainties. These needs are sometimes tied, for example, to their overall economic vulnerabilities that make it difficult for them to access basic health care and welfare. Furthermore, popular religion is typically, and mistakenly, associated with the poor.[47]

On the other hand, reducing experience to economic needs is a narrow view. It focuses only on the demand, as it were. The experiential practicality of popular religion embodies what to us is the operation of God in the here and now. As we argue in the succeeding chapters, dismissing popular piety misses out on the possibility of divine work at play. In his work on God in popular culture, Andrew Greeley insists that "people are sacraments of God."[48] In other words, people's dreams, aspirations, fears, and hopes—all of which drive their yearnings for the divine—reveal "legitimate experience of God, legitimate symbols of God, and legitimate stories of God."[49] It is in this light that the practical rationality of people's Christianity provides a more fundamental rationality, one that is spiritual. The yearnings that people have for God's work are only indicative of deeper longings for a relationship with the divine. In his own work on Catholic youth, Cornelio shows that even though young people have insecurities about their future (which also play out in their spiritual lives), their prayers unravel a relational view of God.[50] In their religious worldview, Christ is a brother, a friend, even a "trash can because [they] get to throw at Him all the dirty things in [them]."[51] This relational view ties in with the first point we made about the authenticity of people's Christianity for its adherents.

Conclusion

This chapter has been about the diversity of lived Christianity in different contexts around the world. To this end, we have spelled out four crucial elements: authenticity, the location of the sacred, the presence and mediation of sacred power, and practical rationality as the basis of people's Christianity.

While our approach to analyzing the state of people's Christianity today has been very sociological, the overall point remains the same: to smell the sheep. The metaphor is very instructive. Sheep are smelly. To smell them deliberately can be repulsive to strangers. Interestingly, the diverse forms of popular religion can also create the same reaction for people, many of whom should not be strangers to Christianity. But religious hierarchies and theological differences have hindered our understanding that underneath people's Christianity are aspirations that are both material and spiritual.

The appeal to smell the sheep is therefore as much an analytical concern as it is a pastoral one. At one level, we have been interested in unravelling the sociological characteristics of people's Christianity. Our approach has been consistent with emerging scholarship on popular religion around the world today. For example, analytical distinctions between sacred and profane do not make sense once people's motives and the location of the sacred are considered. Our starting point was also the assumption that for people, their popular piety is what makes their Catholic identity authentic.

These realizations have a bearing on pastoral work. Interestingly, much of people's Christianity is neither fanatical nor idolatrous. We have argued, for example, for the authenticity of people's Christianity.

At the same time, we have noted that the practical rationality of popular Christianity is not just an economic concern but is also deeply rooted in spirituality or yearnings for the divine. Therefore, lived Christianity embodies worship and people's aspirations for liberation that we explore in the second part.

PART II

READING BETWEEN THE LINES

3

Lived Christianity as Worship

PART 1 GAVE an overview of how Christian communities and individuals live their faith in different contexts throughout the world. This lived Christianity finds expression in diverse practices; many have had an enduring history, others arise from the interaction of Christianity with local contexts, and some have been part of the movement of groups from one context to another.[1]

In part 2, we critically analyze how lived Christianity is approached by two different contemporary perspectives: first, under the rubric of worship; and second, in the context of social transformation.

This chapter, which focuses on lived Christianity as worship, begins with a close reading and general assessment of the *Directory on Popular Piety and the Liturgy: Principles and Guidelines*, the most extensive Catholic document on the subject issued by the Vatican Congregation for Divine Worship and the Discipline of the Sacraments for "episcopal vicars, priests, deacons, and especially for rectors of sanctuaries."[2] Like other official documents issued by offices of the Holy See, it follows the usual genre of such texts, drawing from the rich trove of Christian tradition and written by an official group of officers and consultants. The chapter concludes with a discussion of the Chinese Rites Controversy to illustrate the limitations of considering lived Christianity under the rubric of worship.

Directory on Popular Piety and the Liturgy

The 253-page *Directory* includes introductory documents and its primary text, which is divided into two parts. The first part, "Emerging Trends, History, Magisterium, Theology," has an introduction and three chapters covering relations between liturgy and popular piety in historical perspective and in the church's magisterium, as well as guidelines for the evaluation and renewal of popular piety. The second part, "Guidelines for the Harmonization of Popular Piety with the Liturgy," consists of five chapters, each one focused on specific areas such as the veneration of Mary and the saints, followed by a brief conclusion.

Three central themes regarding popular piety are developed throughout the main text. These are the place, the value, and the evaluation of popular piety. First, the *Directory* differentiates popular piety as communal Christian practices from the generic "popular religiosity" and the specific "popular devotions" and locates its place within Christian worship (*Directory* 8–10). Despite this attempt at clarification, Mark Francis, a specialist on liturgical inculturation, notes that "the historical reality that underlies these terms is much more messy than the definitions seem to suggest," and that these categories are so defined "in terms of their distance or closeness to the liturgy."[3] For this reason, the term *popular piety* is used inclusively in this chapter.

Consequently, lived Christianity becomes most visible in terms of how Christians express their faith—their response to God—through concrete instances of popular piety. This recalls Paul's advice to the Thessalonians: "Pray without ceasing, give thanks in all circumstances; for this is the will of God in Christ Jesus for you" (1 Thess 5:17–18).

Thus, the *Directory*'s publication underscores the Catholic Church's recognition of the spiritual value of popular piety and builds on earlier magisterial documents, particularly the Second Vatican Council's *Sacrosanctum Concilium*. This conciliar constitution on the liturgy already speaks of popular piety's "contribution to living with Christ" (nos. 12–13).[4] But as liturgist James Empereur suggests, theological reflection on and pastoral support for popular piety have been sidelined partly because of the impact of far-reaching liturgical reforms inaugurated by the council and also because of the evolution of certain popular devotions independent of official liturgical practice.[5] These situations of disharmony are what the *Directory* seeks to remedy.

In the manner of official church texts, the *Directory* notes that other documents from different Vatican entities and bishops' conferences have discussed popular piety. For instance, it quotes *Vicesimus Quintus Annus* of John Paul II: "Popular piety can neither be ignored nor treated with indifference or disrespect because of its richness and because in itself it represents a religious attitude in relation to God" (*Directory* 18).

Second, and related to this spiritual richness, the *Directory* highlights the value of popular piety. Though "inspired predominantly not by the Sacred Liturgy but by forms from a particular nation or people or from their culture," forms of popular piety are cherished as "a treasure of the people of God" (no. 9). As such, they promote human values associated with popular religiosity, such as the sense of the sacred and of God's providence and mercy as well as such Christian dispositions as the willingness to do penance or detachment from material things (no. 61).

But more fundamental than the presence of these human and Christian values, the deeper significance of popular piety lies in "that harmonious fusion of the Gospel message with a particular culture" in which "the Gospel message assimilates expressive forms particular to a given culture while also permeating the consciousness of that culture with the content of the Gospel" (no. 63). The *Directory* further adds, "In some cases, this fusion goes so deep that elements proper to the Christian faith become integral elements of the cultural identity of particular nations." Moreover, "the transmission of this cultural heritage from father to son, from generation to generation, also implies the transmission of Christian principles" (no. 63).

For instance, throughout the text, one finds countless references to how popular piety has transmitted profound Christian images and beliefs. Inspired by biblical scenes, Jesus Christ is portrayed as poor and humble (no. 62). Different popular devotions to Mary and other holy men and women express the church's conviction about the Communion of Saints.

As a result of this fusion, popular piety is recognized "for the conservation of the faith itself and in inspiring new efforts at evangelization" (no. 64). More than "an antidote to the sects" and a remedy for Christians deprived of pastoral care, "popular piety is the first and most fundamental form of the faith's 'inculturation'" (nos. 64, 91).

Third, though the value of popular piety is clearly recognized in terms of the faith's inculturation, it "should be continually guided and oriented by the Liturgy, which, in its turn, nourishes the faith through the heart" (no. 91). Thus, much of the document addresses this concern.

Referencing *Sacrosanctum Concilium* again, the *Directory* describes the current problematic as the imbalance in the relations between liturgy and popular piety, in particular, when popular piety is considered contradictory, equal, or a substitute to liturgy (no. 50). Various causes for this imbalance are correctly acknowledged. On the one hand, official ministers look down on popular piety or church liturgy is performed with a ritual formalism wary of being tainted by local elements. On the other hand, popular piety is valued for being open to cultural practices, spontaneous in spirit, and independent of institutional control (nos. 47–59).

To remedy this imbalance, theological principles as well as general and specific practical guidelines are offered for the evaluation and renewal of popular piety. The theological principles described could be summarized in three central themes from church teaching that do not apply only to popular piety.

First, salvation is "a free gift of God, flowing from His mercy, given in sovereign freedom and total gratuity" and involves "a continuous dialogue between God and man" (*Directory* 76). Second, because "the mystery of Christ, especially his Passover of death and Resurrection, is the full and definitive revelation and realization of God's salvific promises," Jesus Christ then becomes "the essential reference point for the faith and prayer life of the people of God" (no. 77). Third, "without the Spirit of Christ there can be neither authentic liturgical worship, nor genuine expressions of popular piety," because it is the Spirit that all worship originates in, draws impetus from and is brought to completion in" (no. 78).

These theological principles have been underscored as relevant for the evaluation and renewal of popular piety because they relate to noted deviations in practice. For instance, some devotees may consider that salvation comes from persistent performance of specific practices according to "some sort of pelagianism" rather than from God's free gift (no. 57).

To these theological principles, the *Directory* adds what it calls "the 'ecclesiological principle' of Christian worship": "Popular piety, as an expression of ecclesial piety, is subject to the general discipline of Christian worship and to the Church's pastoral authority which exercises a role of discernment and authentification in relation to it" (no. 84). With this emphasis on popular piety's link to the church, part 1 of the *Directory* concludes that "popular piety should always be formed as a moment of the dialogue between God and man, through Christ in the Holy Spirit" and notes the resources and resilience of popular piety for renewal (no. 79).

Doctrinal Formulation over Religious Symbolism

Even for an official document from the Vatican, the *Directory* did not generate much discussion in general or in academic publications devoted to theology or religion. One notable exception is the commentary edited by Peter C. Phan and consisting of essays from different theological scholars.[6] Each essay focuses on a particular chapter of the *Directory*, presents the chapter's main points, and then offers some analysis.

The essays contribute toward a deeper understanding of each chapter and give insightful comments on theological and pastoral concerns related to the chapter. They are unanimous in supporting the *Directory*'s recognition of the value of popular piety. The essay by Mark Francis praises its "clear, linear account of the historical relationship between liturgy and popular piety" that "accurately identifies the historical, cultural, and theological factors that led to a rupture between liturgy and popular religious expressions."[7]

Nevertheless, the essays also point to certain inadequacies. For instance, some echo the earlier quoted comment from Empereur on the ambiguity of the distinction between popular piety, religiosity, and devotions. Moreover, Peter Fink questions the prevailing assumption "that the exercise of popular piety comes from below, and it is for this reason that popular piety needs to be evangelized."[8] Thus, despite the *Directory*'s affirmation of popular piety, its repeated insistence on keeping popular piety in line appears disproportionate.

Though helpful, these positive and negative remarks in Phan's anthology point to a more fundamental issue regarding the *Directory*'s approach to popular piety. This issue involves its stress on doctrinal formulation over religious symbolism regarding popular piety. Here the term *symbolism* is intended to cover the figurative use of language, the narrative structure of ritual, the accompaniment of music, and the integral role of material objects and bodily movements.

The *Directory* acknowledges these symbolic elements as part of the language of popular piety that "is characterized by a great variety and richness of bodily, gestural and symbolic expressions: kissing or touching images, places, relics and sacred objects; pilgrimages, processions; going bare-footed or on one's knees; kneeling and prostrating; wearing medals and badges" (no. 15). There is also recognition of the place of music as "the soul of a nation" as well as the importance of local sacred spaces and seasons (nos. 17, 19–20).

However, the overriding concern over these elements of the language of popular piety is that they "ensure the transmission of the truth of the faith together with the greatness of the Christian mysteries" (no. 14). This concern for truthful transmission of the faith is well taken, since popular piety should give "external expression to the heart and to one's commitment to live the Christian life" and "must always be approved by the local Ordinary" (nos. 15, 16).

But the litmus test for conformity appears to be a narrow literal conformity to biblical and doctrinal formulation. Because of the apparent failure of popular piety in this regard, there is the constant call for greater familiarity with the Scripture and ecclesial traditions.

For instance, among those considered as deviations in popular piety is the insufficient reference to the Trinity, especially the Holy Spirit, in prayers (*Directory* 64). Thus "the faithful require instruction on the character of Christian prayer, which is directed to the Father, through the mediation of the Son, in the power of the Holy Spirit" (no. 80).

Similar criticism has been made against forms of popular piety regarding their apparent neglect of the Resurrection. Sections of chapter 4 of the *Directory* single out the common emphasis on the suffering Jesus and the cross: "Devotion to the Cross, however, sometimes requires a certain enlightenment. The faithful should be taught to place the Cross in its essential reference to the Resurrection of Christ: the Cross, the empty tomb, the Death and Resurrection of Christ are indispensable in the Gospel narrative of God's salvific plan" (no. 128).

These comments recall criticisms often made against those from the Global South: liberation theologians who focus on Christ's suffering or artists who depict Christ as an impoverished *campesino* or victim of torture. For instance, Gustavo Gutiérrez's classic *A Theology of Liberation* has been criticized both for using a Peruvian crucifix with a disfigured Christ on its cover and for insisting that "participation in the process of liberation is an obligatory and privileged *locus* for Christian life and reflection."[9] In his survey of critics of liberation theology, Arthur McGovern writes, "The most militant critics of liberation theology accuse it of reducing faith to politics; other critics believe that it 'risks' such a reduction."[10]

This emphasis on the suffering Jesus is not new but has antecedents in the church's tradition, especially during the medieval period. In his historical study, *The Beauty of the Cross*, Richard Viladesau analyzes late medieval theology and art from the likes of Guito and concludes, "The sufferings of Christ became even more central to Christian piety, and forms of devotion that focused on them multiplied....Moreover, this devotion was increasingly focused on Christ's suffering itself, and increasingly invited believers both to identify with that suffering and to regard themselves in its light as sinners, and hence as the cause of the passion and death of God's Son."[11]

However, Viladesau also adds that even in this emphasis on Christ's suffering, "the resurrection is not entirely forgotten, even if it remains in the background (frequently literally so, in the form of the golden or decorated panels on which the crucifixion is portrayed, and which remind us that this drama is God's act of salvation)."[12] Thus, such focus on Jesus's passion does not indicate denial of his resurrection but solidarity with those still suffering as well as hope in Christ's redemptive power.

Criticism over this focus merely shows the dominant emphasis on doctrinal formulation in the evaluation of popular piety and the insufficient attention to the symbolic nature of popular piety. What is deemed missing then are literal or visual equivalents of declarative statements of doctrine.

Given this, the *Directory* considers the importance of "formation of both clergy and laity...[as] a means of resolving many of the reasons underlying the imbalances between the Liturgy and popular piety" (no. 59). But the greater emphasis lies on those engaged in popular piety as perennial objects of evangelization, because of the implication that popular piety is bereft of any theological foundations.

Historical studies of many forms of popular piety deny this absence of theological substance. The *Directory* itself mentions how pastors "have recommended and encouraged them, or guided and corrected them or simply tolerated them" and how some have been "erected by the Apostolic See, or...have been recommended by the same Apostolic See throughout the ages" or "undertaken by order of the bishops according to customs or books lawfully approved" (no. 72). Given this involvement of pastors who have undergone theological formation, it cannot be said, then, that theological influence is absent in popular piety.

An excellent illustration is found in the Philippine *Pasyon* (Passion) tradition of chanting or dramatizing the history of salvation during Holy Week. Its text, written by an unknown author and first published in 1814, consists of more than 2,500 quatrains originally composed in Tagalog and subsequently translated into other Philippine languages.[13]

Rene Javellana's account of its complex textual history shows the extent and depth of its theological sources, drawn from the influence of Spanish and Tagalog antecedents, and the redaction of its clerical editors.[14] The *Pasyon* text lifts sections from these antecedents, especially the 1703 poem by native Gaspar Aquino de Belen, and contains biblical details or quotations from the Latin Vulgate, sections of Catholic liturgy and songs, and references to such authors as the Council of Trent Jesuit theologian Alonso Salmeron (1512–85).[15] Through these diverse source materials, most probably accessed from known medieval collections such as Josef Pinton's *Compendio Historico de la Religion*, the *Pasyon* text carries a rich trove of medieval theology. One finds, for instance, the theological distinction between Adam and Eve's *paraiso terrenal* (earthly paradise)[16] and the good thief's *paradiso* (heaven)[17] or the medieval view that Mary's salvation came through the blood shed by the infant Jesus at his circumcision.[18]

Though such medieval theological subtleties surely escape ordinary chanters of the text then and today, they serve to illustrate how forms of popular piety often have profound theological foundations. Thus, the question regarding popular forms no longer pertains to the lack of such foundations but to what religious value earlier theological views have for today's faith. While the *Directory* strongly affirms the value of the church's heritage, one still needs to determine this relevance on a case-to-case basis. But to answer whether the *Pasyon* tradition and its text—which have been profoundly shaped by medieval theological concerns—speak to and express the faith of its contemporary chanters, one would have to understand the nuances of its symbolic language.

Separating Popular Piety from Liturgy and from Life

The second fundamental issue "between the lines of the *Directory*" is its strict separation of popular piety from liturgy and from life.

Popular piety and liturgy are clearly distinguished given the perceived lack of harmony between them. The *Directory* quotes from church documents from Vatican II onward in affirming "the Sacred Liturgy" as "the summit of the Church's life" (no. 2). Thus "every liturgical celebration, because it is an action of Christ the Priest and of his Body, which is the Church, is a sacred action surpassing all others. No other action of the Church can equal its efficacy by the same title or to the same degree" (no. 11).

Thus, "while sacramental actions are *necessary* to life in Christ, the various forms of popular piety are properly *optional*" and, though recognized as a form of worship, are seen as limited in scope and value (nos. 11, 12). Given this strict separation between liturgy and popular piety as the basis for the primacy of the liturgy, the *Directory* fails to provide a differentiated view of the structure and development of the liturgy itself.

This failure is first reflected in the *Directory*'s tendency "to name the liturgical life of the church simply as 'the Sacred Liturgy.'"[19] Although the document appropriately reiterates *Sacrosanctum Concilium*'s insistence on the liturgical centrality of the celebration of the paschal mystery of Christ, this Vatican II document itself mentions liturgical forms other than the Eucharist that are related to the paschal mystery—the other sacraments, sacramental, or the Liturgy of the Hours. Without recognizing these other liturgical forms, "the full significance of both the Constitution on the Sacred Liturgy and its post conciliar reform is hardly represented simply by using the term 'Sacred Liturgy' to capture it."[20] Moreover in keeping with this inadequate differentiation of the liturgy, the Directory also glosses over the historical development of these liturgical forms. One does not need a comprehensive history of the liturgy along the lines of Joseph Jungmann's two-volume classic *The Mass of the Roman Rite* to witness its complex historical development.[21]

Even the broad outline of this history in the *Directory*'s first chapter beginning with the period of Christian antiquity suffices. It notes that "the Apostolic and post apostolic periods are marked by a profound fusion of the cultic realities which are now called Liturgy and popular piety" (no. 23). Moreover, what it observes about the development of the liturgy in the fourth century could be taken as generally applicable:

> The local Churches, guided by clear pastoral and evangelizing principles, did not hesitate to absorb into the Liturgy certain purified solemn and festive cultic elements deriving from the pagan world. These were regarded as capable of moving the minds and imaginations of the people who felt drawn toward them. Such forms, now placed at the service of the mystery of worship, were seen as neither contrary to the Gospel nor to the purity of true Christian worship. Rather, there was a realization that only in the worship of Christ, true God and true Saviour, could many cultic expressions, previously attributed to false gods and false saviours, become true cultic expressions, even though these had derived from man's deepest religious sense. (no. 24)

Given this, Francis insists that while the liturgy's focus on and celebration of the paschal mystery is central to its identity, the symbols that are used for this celebration, the way in which the celebration is ordered, and the emphasis placed on certain elements of the faith are conditioned by the historical and cultural context in which the liturgy is celebrated. In short, the liturgy has often been just as influenced by its cultural context as popular piety has been. It is imperative that the liturgy-as-cultural-product—those "elements subject to change" mentioned in the Constitution on Sacred Liturgy—be acknowledged and not confused with the "divinely instituted, immutable elements."[22]

In addition, Fink states, "At the very least, the way in which the living presence of Christ is presented, and the way our liturgy accomplishes what Christ intends, needs in some way to be articulated if the relationship between pious practices and the liturgy is to be properly understood."[23]

Thus, it is precisely in recognizing that both the liturgy and popular piety are shaped by cultural elements that disharmony between them could be avoided. However, the *Directory* instead insists on "the objective difference between pious exercises and devotional practices" (no. 12) and avoiding any "mixture or admixture of these two forms of piety" so "that no hybrid, or confused forms emerge from mixing Liturgy and pious exercises" (no. 74). In the end, such a strict separation between liturgy and popular piety presents an inadequate picture of popular piety and liturgy.

Related to, though distinct from, this strict separation is the more fundamental issue of the relation of both liturgy and popular piety to life. Once again drawing inspiration from recent magisterial documents from Vatican II onward, the *Directory* does not deny the relationship of liturgy to the rest of Christian life. But neither does it develop this relationship; it does not even mention *Sacrosanctum Concilium*'s reference to church activity beyond liturgy, such as "works of charity, piety and the apostolate, thus making it clear that the Christ's faithful, though not of this world, are to be lights of the world and are to glorify the Father before men" (*SC* 9).

The *Directory* has more to say about popular piety's relation to life. On the personal level, it emphasizes individual dispositions, such as reverence for life and family, that contribute to true worship; regarding culture, it recognizes social practices that are integrated to piety. For instance, it mentions that "popular piety can express an awareness of the justice and mercy of God the Father, and of His care for the poor and lowly, and it can proclaim that He commends the good and rewards those who live properly and honestly, while abhorring evil and casting away from Himself those who obstinately follow the path of hatred, violence, injustice and deceit" (no, 79).

However, the relation of popular piety to "the rest of life" transcends this awareness of God's love, especially for the poor and the suffering expressed in popular piety. As *Sacrosanctum Concilium* and more recent church documents articulate, all piety draws from and feeds into the totality of personal and communal life; thus, their relationship is dynamic and dialectic.

The *Directory*'s insufficient emphasis on this dynamic and dialectic relationship lies in its narrow view of popular piety as cultic. Unlike rites that are clearly bounded with a delineated beginning and ending, forms of popular piety have no such definite boundaries. They grow organically from and spill into ordinary life activities. For instance, communal preparations and celebrations surround practices of popular piety, and one is hard put to say that the usual meals that often accompany forms of popular piety are not an integral part of these devotional practices.

The Chinese Rites Controversy

Close reading of the *Directory* has shown the church's recognition of the value of popular piety as well as its concern for harmonization with the liturgy, especially as described by *Sacrosanctum Concilium* from Vatican II and other recent texts. Given the particularities of its literary genre and historical context, its contribution in terms of calling attention to and inviting reflection on popular piety deserves to be more widely recognized.

At the same time, reading between the lines of the *Directory* has also uncovered the inadequacy in its view of popular piety as worship and insufficiently addressed issues in its approach. In particular, this view and its related approach fail to account for the symbolic nature integral to popular piety and the seamless link of popular piety to the totality of Christian life.

Within the context of this critical reading, the well-known and much researched Chinese Rites Controversy associated with Jesuit Matteo Ricci (1552–1610) provides an excellent illustration of the consequences of considering lived Christianity primarily as cultic worship.[24]

In summary, the controversy focuses on the rites of venerating ancestors through bowing and incense, and on whether these ritual actions constitute idolatrous allegiance to other powers beyond the Christian God. According to Sangkeun Kim's masterful work, Ricci's acceptance of the rites generated intense and bitter reactions, negative as well as positive, from the church—his missionary contemporaries, Jesuit and other religious, superiors in Asia and Rome—as well as from outside—Confucian scholars, for example.[25] The conflict generated by the controversy is reflected in its extensive influence, even on eighteenth-century Protestant missions, and even the diversity of official verdicts: prohibition of the rites was issued by Pope Clement IX in 1704 and reaffirmed by Pope Benedict XIV in 1742, but was reversed by Pope Pius XII in 1939.

But beyond these polemics or the evaluation of Ricci's missionary strategy, its significance in relation to popular piety lies in the use of the doctrinal as the primary norm for the assessment of the rites. With this stress on conformity with Christian belief in God, the symbolic language of the rites as well as their profound insertion into Chinese social life received little consideration.

In contrast, recent studies indicate the prominent place of the rites within the sociopolitical milieu and the symbolic world of the Chinese. First, these rites of venerating ancestors were clearly more than just ritual practices, having developed from China's ancient beginnings and interacted with enduring cultural traditions such as Confucianism. Though they have taken various forms and relations with these traditions, their integral place in Chinese culture and society is beyond doubt. William Lakos comments, "Ancestor worship highlighted the family and kin relationships, as a model for society. Ancestor worship and ritual also provided the individual and society with a set of values, especially in relation to social unity, such as order, benevolence, harmony, and reciprocity. It provided links with the dead and gave rise and force to an ontological reality which supported both the now and the then."[26] Thus it "not only ordered the socio-political realm, but also the cosmic" and "eventually provided the grounds for the most enduring social system in world history."[27]

Given this profound role and connection, the Chinese Rites Controversy could not primarily be, as many within the church then thought, a theological question regarding their compatibility with Christian belief. As Kim notes in his thorough account of the controversy's history, imperial rulers as well as local lords became involved, not only because of their relations with European missionaries but also because of the conflicts the controversy generated among and between Chinese Christians and Confucian scholars. Moreover, aside from power relations, what appeared to be at stake in these conflicts was the social ethos of filial piety that bound Chinese society through performance of these rites. Second, the controversy also proved to be the proverbial "tip of the iceberg" in terms of the symbolic world of the Chinese. Among others, a central issue during the controversy was the Chinese name for the Christian God.[28] Ricci's acceptance of the ancestral rites was based on his discovery of *Shangti* in the Chinese Classics and his subsequent "Thomistic enterprise" of showing "an analogical *similitudo* between the Christian *Deus* and the Confucian *Shangti*."[29] But given the long and complex genealogy of this term in Chinese thought and life, objections came not only from Catholic voices but also from anti-Christian Confucian intellectuals, who insisted on "the difference between the Confucian *Shangti* and the Christian *Shangti*."[30]

These objections and conflicts indicate how deeply embedded the rites and their basis on *Shangti* were in the symbolic world of the Chinese. Jacques Gernet even links it with the linguistic peculiarities of the Chinese language: in contrast to Western languages "founded upon categories considered to be universal and…concerned with abstraction and ideas that are stable," Chinese morphology "recognizes only functional classifications and oppositions."[31] Thus the Chinese language is merely concerned "not with 'yes' or 'no,' being or non-being, but contraries which succeed, combine with and complement one another, not with eternal realities but with potentialities and tendencies, phases of flowering or decline."[32]

However, like the link to Chinese sociopolitical milieu, this profound connection of the rites to the Chinese symbolic world was not paid sufficient attention to in the controversy.

It would be moot to surmise whether the resolution of Chinese Rites Controversy would have been different if these fundamental issues had been addressed. But the legacy of the controversy underscores the inadequacy of seeing lived religion under the rubric of worship and the need for an integral perspective that speaks its symbolic language and values its links to "the rest of life."

4

Lived Christianity as Promotion of Liberation

ANOTHER RECENT PERSPECTIVE on lived Christianity focuses on its relation to liberation. This perspective first attracted attention with the emergence of Latin American theology beginning in the 1970s and has subsequently been recognized as a fundamental theological dimension. Thus, this dimension has remained current in theological discussions and official church documents from many quarters, but especially from the Global South and those sectors that profoundly experience the need for and the urgency of liberation.

This chapter examines the link between liberation and popular religion and builds upon the insightful analysis from Michael Candelaria's *Popular Religion and Liberation* and Orlando Espín's *The Faith of the People*.[1] While Candelaria's primary interest in popular religion lies in its liberating role, if any, and Espín's as *locus theologicus*, this chapter focuses on whether the liberationist perspective offers a comprehensive theological account of lived Christianity. It does not undertake a complete analysis of this perspective as exemplified in either its Latin American expression—commonly referred to as "liberation theology"—or in theologies of liberation from other contexts. Our focus here is whether this perspective takes note of the various dimensions of how Christians live their faith. Just as the previous chapter explored the perspective of lived Christianity as worship, this chapter offers a critical analysis of the liberationist account of lived Christianity.

This chapter is divided into five sections. The first discusses the emergence of the two currents of Latin American liberation theology—general liberation theology and the Theology of the People—and their impact on the approach to popular religion. Drawing from representative texts of liberation theologians, the next two sections discuss the analysis of the locus of both currents and the subjects of liberation and its implications regarding popular religion. The final section presents a general assessment of the liberationist perspective on popular religion.

Emergence of Liberation Theology with Two Currents[2]

The status of lived Christianity vis-à-vis liberation cannot be understood apart from the tortuous journey of Latin American liberation theology with its multiple historical and intellectual strands. Religion and poverty are characteristic of Latin America, and, as Candelaria comments, "these two factors, piety and oppression, serve as theological and pastoral points of departure."[3]

Before irrupting on the global theological stage in the 1970s and 1980s, Latin American liberation theology had been brewing around the time of Vatican II (1962–65). Since the 1960s, many of its pioneers belonged to "Church and Society"—a group of engaged Catholics and Protestants of different nationalities who met regularly to examine the place of Christianity with its colonial legacy under the light of the Spirit informing the council.[4] Educated in Latin American and European institutions and now teaching at seminaries and universities throughout the subcontinent, they were conversant with European intellectual traditions and regional issues involving religion and society.

Because of this common purpose and similar intellectual background, they received Vatican II with keen interest and sharp insight. They were aware of deep-seated differences between the Vatican curia and various nonofficial groups pushing for change. Of particular interest were those identified by Hilari Raguer as the "Central European bloc," or "World Alliance," and the "Church of the Poor."[5] The first group—composed of bishops from Central Europe and Scandinavia plus others "who shared their open-minded understanding of the Council"[6]—wielded great influence throughout the council because of its "very stable nucleus" consisting of Cardinals Josef Frings (Cologne), Franz König (Vienna), Achille Liénart (Lille), Leo Suenens (Brussels), and Bernard Alfrink (Utrecht).[7] The other group, the Church of the Poor, consisted of some French-speaking and Latin American participants, all inspired by post–World War II social Catholicism, especially in France. With Brazilian Archbishop Helder Camara and French-born Bishop Georges Mercier of Algeria as voices during the council, this group "raised three main problems: (1) development of the poor countries; (2) evangelization of the poor and workers; and (3) giving the Church once more its poor 'face.'"[8] Thus they underlined the integral link between the church and the poor as well as between charity and just social structures.[9]

These complex questions, brought to the council from diverse theological perspectives and sociogeographical locations, were taken to heart by those from Church and Society as well as by others in the Latin American churches. They grappled with these questions in relation to the Latin American situation, and their response to the historic council found expression in what would become liberation theology. As Gerard Whelan rightly states, "Liberation theology represents a distinctively Latin American application of Vatican II."[10]

Within this horizon, Latin American liberation theology is born with "two interrelated parts, one directed toward the Christian tradition, the other directed toward society. The former included a rereading of Christianity from history's underside....The latter part included the use of the social sciences."[11]

These shaping influences give rise to various forms, but liberation theology eventually separates into two distinct currents, which have been given various labels. For Cardinal Walter Kasper, one is "generally better known to us [from an analysis of socioeconomic and political relations or...from antagonisms in society]" and the other not so,[12] while E. Jorda identifies liberation theology in the sociopolitical and the cultural realms.[13] These currents have emerged in relation to liberation theology's orientation toward society, particularly in the different tools they employ to understand their contexts. Such differences became predominant in different parts of the subcontinent and have accounted for their corresponding views on popular religion.

GENERAL LIBERATION THEOLOGY

The first and the "better-known" current—here referred to as general liberation theology—encompasses works of prominent native and foreign-born authors originally written in Spanish but soon translated into other languages.[14] Its many proponents, such as Uruguayan Juan Luis Segundo and the Brazilian brothers Leonardo and Clodovis Boff, were deeply involved with *comunidades de base* among the many poor; others, such as Argentinian Enrique Dussel, were associated with particular political movements and thus suffered imprisonment or exile. The group included many Catholic clerics, such as Peruvian Gustavo Gutiérrez, some members of Protestant churches, and a few women theologians.

In their engagement with their social context, they "sought to better understand the causes of oppression" and then "to develop 'historical projects'"—that is, "models of political and economic organization."[15]

Given "a swell of small but militant revolutionary movements" but also "the beginnings of repressive military rule in many countries of Latin America,"[16] liberation theologians drew from their European intellectual background of the "radical Enlightenment"—"more identified with the French *philosophes* and with Jean-Jacques Rousseau" and the political thought of Karl Marx.[17] As a result, these proponents of general liberation theology "rather universally and staunchly oppose capitalism and favor some sort of socialism."[18]

This opposition to capitalism and acceptance of some form of socialism proved to be the most controversial issue for general liberation theology. On the one hand, the nascent desire for profound and even radical reform within church and society from the 1960s facilitated broad acceptance of general liberation theology, including its historical project. Its themes were recognized by official Catholic voices, especially the regional bishops' conference, *Consejo Episcopal Latinoamericano* (CELAM) at Medellín (Colombia) in 1968 and at Puebla (Mexico) in 1979, as well as by theologians and church leaders from other contexts.

However, unforeseen events from the 1980s onward produced a zeitgeist unsupportive of general liberation theology. As Tombs recounts, "The fall of the Berlin Wall [1989], the collapse of the Eastern bloc, and the electoral defeat of the Nicaraguan Sandinistas in February

1990" led to "the apparent triumph of free markets in Latin America" and subsequently in the general global order.[19]

Within the Catholic Church, the 1978 election of Pope John Paul II from Communist Poland facilitated what some have called the decline, even the death, of liberation theology as a movement.[20] Under Cardinal Joseph Ratzinger's tenure from 1981 onward, the Vatican Congregation for the Doctrine of the Faith (CDF) investigated such prominent liberation theologians as Leonardo Boff, Sobrino, and Gutiérrez, and issued two critical statements dated 1984 and 1986 respectively. The first and more unfavorable document criticized general liberation theology's alleged reduction of Christian salvation to political liberation and its uncritical embrace of ideologies and practices inspired by the Marxist tradition. Moreover, the Vatican's intervention at the 1992 Santo Domingo (Dominican Republic) meeting of CELAM, now dominated by bishops appointed by Pope John Paul II, ensured a document untainted by any liberationist perspective.

Partly in response to these historical changes and paradigm shifts, general liberation theologians clarified their views and proceeded to address new perspectives from spirituality, feminism, and ecology. Moreover, those from analogous social situations in Asia and Africa and from marginalized sectors in industrialized countries incorporated or modified insights from general liberation theology. For instance, Asian responses, notably Sri Lankan Aloysius Pieris's *Asian Theology of Liberation* (1988), point to integral differences between Latin America and their contexts, particularly the presence of significant cosmic traditions and deeply rooted world religions.[21] Comments from Africa bring out the need to describe liberation in relation to traditional cultures and religions.

As a result of this tortuous journey, one could say that general liberation theology has undergone transformation. With its disentanglement from recent Marxist-inspired historical projects, the trope of liberation itself has been broadly accepted in contemporary theological reflection and official church teaching, leading some to speak of the "re-invention" of liberation theology.[22]

THEOLOGY OF THE PEOPLE

The second current, referred to as Theology of the People (*teología del pueblo*), was contemporaneous with the first but remained generally unknown beyond Latin America because of its focus on the Argentinian sociocultural situation. However, it has recently attracted wider attention because of its formative influence on the thought and practice of the Argentinian Pope Francis.

In contrast to the first current's use of social analysis inspired by various iterations of the Marxist tradition, the Theology of the People organically grew out of the Argentinian situation and employed a liberation perspective shaped by prominent local scholars and other intellectual strands of modern European thought.

Argentina had been characterized by extensive urbanization and ethnic homogeneity, just like Uruguay—the context of Segundo's general liberation theology.[23] But these contexts differed significantly regarding church-state relations. While Uruguay's secularization from the late nineteenth century onward brought about the eventual disestablishment of Christianity within the public sphere, Roman Catholicism remained prominent in Argentinian society. Aside from its overwhelming majority, its ethos continued to influence civic life through official and informal links with sociopolitical forces.

This involvement of the Catholic Church in national affairs is reflected in its shifting relations with Juan Perón throughout his three separate terms as president. During the first term (1946–51), the church openly supported him because of his acceptance of papal encyclicals as social policy and his opposition to legalizing divorce. But during his turbulent second term (1951–55), which ended in his deposition by military coup, the church became critical of his economic policies and increasing authoritarianism; in turn, he attacked the church for its support of militant labor unions. After a long exile, Perón returned in 1973 for a third term that was cut short by his death the following year. Support still came from an unlikely collaboration of various forces: "A sort of left-wing neo-nationalism followed the apparent internal logic of the 'Church of the poor' and the 'People of God,' in which the poor were identified with the working class and the workers with Peronism."[24] But beyond these shifts in Argentinian church-state relations, what was most significant was the underlying entanglement of Christianity and nation that provided an important backdrop for the Theology of the People.

Furthermore, the intellectual and cultural background of Argentinian scholars proved crucial for this second current of liberation theology. Instead of the radical Enlightenment and its Marxist progeny that general liberation theology employed, "the spirit of democratic romanticism…found its way into Argentina at the end of the nineteenth century" through the ideas of the German thinker Karl Christian Friedrich Krause (1781–1832).[25] This background shaped the thought of those engaged in this second current of liberation theology.

Among its known proponents were Lucio Gera, Juan Carlos Scannone, Fernando Boasso, and Aldo Buntig.[26] If Gutiérrez is considered the father of the first current, the diocesan priest Gera is similarly regarded for the second. His student years in Europe exposed him not only to the Young Christian Workers movement but also, more significantly, to the theological legacy of the nineteenth-century Catholic Tübingen School and particularly to the thought of Johann Adam Möhler (1796–1831), whose teaching about the spirit of the people would be echoed in the Argentinian current of liberation theology.[27] These influences shaped Gera's reflections on Latin American poverty and piety so much so that he refused to sign CELAM's final document at Medellín due to "an unacceptable embrace of Marxism."[28]

The Theology of the People turns instead to popular thought to understand society. For it, Latin American intellectual thought "is systematic and tends to be crystallized in encyclopedic form," but popular thought "moves in the sphere of everyday life"—of the emotional, which is "the realm of the symbolic, the unrational and pertains to popular culture, religion and wisdom."[29]

Hence the Theology of the People, like general liberation theology ever committed to the liberation of society, involves "jettisoning ahistoric ideological conceptions of Christianity and transforming theology by means of a historical commitment to 'the transformation of the world and of oneself.'"[30] Its *locus theologicus* is thus found in popular culture and its expressions in art and religion.[31]

This brief overview of the emergence of the two currents of liberation theology notes their common commitment to social transformation in Latin America as well as the differences that arise from diverse historical contexts and intellectual traditions. These differences become pronounced in the corresponding tools they employ for social analysis and would have profound implications in their understanding of Christianity as lived by the people.

Lived Christianity and the Locus of Liberation

These two currents, general liberation theology and the Argentinian Theology of the People, could not ignore popular religion in their critical reflection on Latin American contexts. As liberation theologians, proponents of both are equally committed to the liberation of peoples through the transformation of their societies. In these societies, however, the majority of people are baptized, and their usual religious practice is constituted from diverse sources such as indigenous traditions, the colonial Catholic legacy, and recent Protestant evangelism.

José Miguez Bonino, an Argentinian Protestant liberation theologian, lists two reasons why popular religion cannot be overlooked or lightly dismissed by its critics: (1) popular religion is a mass phenomenon and must be reckoned with to integrate the masses into the struggle for liberation; and (2) political and religious groups from the Right and the Left try to manipulate popular religion toward their political and social goals.[32]

This section examines texts from both currents that express their views on popular Christianity and then underlines their differences. To begin, it employs Harvey Cox's seminal essay that states, "Even at its inception there was an active discussion in the liberation theology movement about the significance of *religión popular*."[33]

In reading between the lines of these texts, one finds two fundamental questions behind their respective views. The first question about the locus of liberation concerns the relation between popular religion and liberation—in particular, whether popular religion offers a locus for liberation. In the words of Segundo Galilea, perhaps the liberation theologian most interested in popular religion, "Is [popular religion] a valid starting point for liberation? Does it lead to conformity and alienation? Can a critical and developing consciousness be developed from folk religion, or must it always be a stage of development that has to be surpassed?"[34]

The second question focuses on the subjects of liberation, that is, on which "people" bring about liberation. Responses to these questions from both currents differ because of their use of different approaches to social analysis. These differences similarly shape their views on popular religion.

According to Cox, general liberation theology took a highly critical view of popular religion from the outset. He points to José Miguez Bonino's early essay, which echoes a CELAM report: "The religiosity of poverty does not work to change life. It is well known that such Catholicism strengthens a dualistic vision of reality and, therefore, a religious attitude alien to the tasks of this world."[35] Moreover, "such popular Catholicism reinforces the social system with all its injustices, contradictions, and forms of oppression."[36]

In this highly critical view of popular religion expressed by liberation theologians and in some official texts from CELAM, popular religion is negatively characterized in terms of the following elements: (1) fatalism that "encourages persons to accept the situation in which they find themselves as the will of God or as according to the order of creation"; (2) individualism that puts "the attempt to 'save my own individual soul' at the expense of corporate or cooperative action in society"; (3) "finding spurious solutions to genuine human dilemmas"; (4) "blessing of intergroup and interclass harmony through an emphasis on love and reconciliation"; and (5) "immersion in the popular religious mind-scape" that hinders participation in the development of the wider society."[37] All these elements "are, in the rapid evolution of society, the expression of alienated groups—that is, of groups that live in a depersonalized, conformist, and noncritical manner and do not make efforts to change society."[38] Furthermore, "this kind of religiosity is maintained and encouraged by the prevailing structures of which the church is a part."[39]

According to this critique then, popular religion does not provide the locus for liberation and even lends legitimacy to the unjust status quo. This view is rooted in social analysis shaped by the Marxist tradition as found, for example, in Segundo's acclaimed 1976 book, *Liberation of Theology*.

Segundo's work explicates his analysis of the place and role of popular religion: "Religion is intricately bound up with the whole system of relationships that governs the mentality of the people. So true is this that one can say that the religious factors have ceased to be autonomous at the very least, and perhaps even religious at all."[40] Religion considered as "superstructure" cannot be a liberating force unless fundamental social structures are changed: "Existing reality must undergo a transformation before a religious structure, which was originally accepted by the masses for the objective motive of fitting themselves into the existing system, can be turned into a force for 'unsettling' that system."[41]

Notwithstanding this view of the Christianity commonly lived throughout Latin America, Segundo does not altogether dismiss popular religion and proposes an approach of focusing on societal change. Rejecting what he refers to as typological and populist approaches, he turns to Galilea's succinct but comprehensive analysis of popular religion. In *The Challenge of Popular Religiosity*, Galilea recognizes many aspects of popular Christianity: its integrating cultural power, its inevitable transformation due to forces of modernization, and its multidimensional relation to the gospel and the church.[42]

Moreover, though structural transformation remains the locus of liberation, Galilea affirms the significance of culture and religion for this transformation. He enumerates forms of cultural liberation that even the church could engage in: (1) "relativizing the religious expressions that 'popular Catholicism' tends to repeat cyclically and to absolutize into an enslaving thing"; (2) "integrating into individualistic religious expressions the original dimension of the Christian religion which has to do with communitarian solidarity and fraternity as essential features of any religious act"; and (3) "revealing the element of protest against injustice and oppression that exists in religious attitudes."[43]

Given these possible forms of liberation, Galilea states a more nuanced view of popular religion: "Liberation theologians are agreed in seeing the religion of the people as basically Christian—therefore containing a liberating dynamism, though at present ambiguous and conditioned by oppression and therefore capable of deviating and playing an alienating role."[44] General liberation theology, then, recognizes its potential for liberation but still identifies the locus of liberation in the transformation of unjust economic and political structures.

While just as committed to social transformation as the first current, the Theology of the People does not employ social analysis inspired by the Marxist tradition and thus offers a different view of the locus of liberation and of popular religion in general.

As a result of this difference based on differing intellectual traditions and sociopolitical contexts, the Theology of the People locates the praxis of liberation elsewhere. For Scannone, its foremost proponent, it is decidedly the historical praxis of the people that is "concerned both with liberation and with the creation of their own culture"[45] and that constitutes "an anticipatory foretaste and sign of God's definitive salvation, a sign of his saving action being manifested in history."[46] In Candelaria's analysis, it refers to "the history of the Latin American struggle for freedom and independence....Consequently, praxis is rooted in Latin American history and in its Christian tradition."[47]

Thus, for the Theology of the People, popular culture and popular religion become an important locus of liberation, and their analysis involves a different set of tools. Scannone's recent essay on his former student Pope Francis characterizes them as follows:

> (1) use of historical-cultural analysis (*el análisis histórico-cultural*), privileging it over structural social analysis (*el análisis socio-cultural*) without discarding the latter; (2) employment of more synthetic and hermeneutical sciences such as history, culture, and religion (as complements to more analytical and structural sciences) as a form of mediation to get to know reality and to transform it; (3) rooting of such scientific mediations in a sapiential knowledge and discernment for the sake of the 'affective connaturality that love gives' (*EG* 125), which, in turn, confirms their scientific character; and (4) taking a critical distance from the Marxist method of social analysis and its categories of understanding and practical strategies.[48]

Scannone grounds the use of these tools in an epistemological rupture from "modern rationality, its logos, and worldview" that questions its episteme and "unmask[s] its ideological instrumentalization."[49] What he calls the hermeneutic locale—the privileged sphere for theology, philosophy, and pastoral strategy—is popular culture with its religious dimension affecting all other spheres of culture.

Given this philosophical framework as basis for its social analysis, the Theology of the People takes a more positive view of popular Catholicism. This theology, in Kasper's words, is "a theology of the people and of culture. In doing so, it does not want to lecture the people, but rather it wants to listen to the people's wisdom. Therefore, a higher value is assigned to popular piety."[50] At the same time, it does not overlook existing social antitheses. Scannone insists that popular religion "is an expression of authentic Christian faith inherited from the past and received from the preaching of the first missionaries. It should continue to be evangelized but in terms of its own proper cultural values."[51]

Thus, the Theology of the People views liberation and the evangelization of culture as intimately connected. According to Candelaria's analysis, it sees that "liberation is primarily cultural, that is, freeing Latin Americans fully to realize their true being....Popular culture, recognized as a fruit of evangelization, needs only to be revitalized, its values of faith rediscovered."[52]

Popular Catholicism, therefore, is deemed valuable because it is the people "which discovers the epiphany of God in its life, celebrates it, expresses it in myths and symbols, seeks it in the form of hope, struggle, or utopia," making it "possible to trace an itinerary toward God using a hermeneutic of these symbols, myths, fiestas, rites, struggles, and utopias."[53]

Through this hermeneutic that puts a premium on religious symbols, Scannone sees not only the potential of cultural resistance but also the possibility of humanizing modern rationality. The capacity of popular wisdom for vital synthesis gives it the potential for integrating popular culture and modern society. Moreover, popular cultural values can be conducive to liberation and could eventually make a genuine contribution to the authentic liberation of Latin American peoples.

The contrasting views on popular religion of the two currents of liberation theology arise from where they place the locus of liberation. Using Marxist-inspired approaches to social analysis, general liberation theology locates it in the transformation of socioeconomic structures. The Theology of the People sees this locus in popular culture. On the one hand, although both currents do not ignore popular religion, the first current values popular religion only as a strategic step toward structural transformation. On the other hand, the Theology of the People considers popular religion as the historical presence of God in the concrete history of the people.

Lived Christianity and the Subjects of Liberation

The second fundamental and arguably more central question behind the relation of popular religion to liberation involves who undertakes liberation. Though related to issues regarding the use of the term *popular* discussed in chapter 1, this issue implicates the specific role of agency in and therefore the identification of the subjects of the process of liberation.

Given that the Christian majority in Latin America practices forms of popular religion, this question is not only unavoidable but also crucial. Here, the crux lies in which "people" in Latin American contexts would be the historical agents of liberation.

Both currents of Latin American liberation theology confront this question first by analyzing the semantic associations of the term *people* and then pinpointing which meaning they employ. Scannone acknowledges the double meaning of the term—the entire people as a nation or the lower classes and popular social sectors comprising the nation—but opts for the first sense, that is, a nation's people "starting from the plural unity of a common culture, rooted in a common history, and projected forward toward a shared common good."[54]

As Candelaria stresses, Scannone's understanding of *people* refers to "an 'organic community' or 'people-nation,' such as the 'Argentine People' or the 'Uruguayan People,'" and "functions as a 'matrix of intelligibility' for interpreting national history, culture, religion, and nationalist movements like Artiguism and Peronism."[55]

This meaning, found in the Argentinian bishops' statements then and in Pope Francis's current discourse, is based on "the notion of the 'people of God' from Vatican II and its interrelationship with various peoples, especially the people of Argentina."[56] Scannone further notes that this inclusive meaning of "people" does not only "promote the emergence of the laity within the church, but also the inclusion of the church in the historical course of peoples inasmuch as they were subjects of history and culture; and, thanks to their inculturated faith, they were also both recipients and agents of evangelization."[57]

Moreover, since the bearers of popular culture are the many poor, whose interests involve the historical project of justice and peace, "therefore, in Latin America, at least *de facto*, the option for the poor coincides with the option for culture. This is probably also the case *de jure*, because the poor are those most likely to reveal the common culture of their people."[58] Thus, institutional and structural injustice is understood as a betrayal of this unity by one part of the whole and thus becomes a force opposed to the people (*antipueblo*).[59]

For the Theology of the People, therefore, the subjects of liberation are the people themselves, understood in its most inclusive sense and acknowledged as the poor majority. In Candelaria's assessment, this "conception of people ends in identifying a nation-state with the people" and comes close to falling into narrow, even Peronist, nationalism. Nevertheless, it "identifies the poor as the backbone of the country" and the people remain "the subjects of their own religion, culture, wisdom, and historical project of liberation."[60]

In contrast to the Theology of the People that focuses on the majority population as subjects of liberation, general liberation theology segments this general category of "people." In his semantic analysis of related vocabulary, Segundo contrasts the following sets of terms within "the people": "majority" or "masses," on one hand, and "minority" or "elite," on the other. He notes further how "such words…are neutral in themselves; they are the product of statistics that anyone can verify. But they are wielded as arguments in themselves, often without any line of reasoning and in direct contradiction to the attitudes and ideological systems that are supposedly being defended."[61] To avoid such pejorative associations, for instance, the title of a CELAM document at Medellín was changed from *Pastoral de masas* to *Pastoral popular*.[62] Given the complications arising from such connotations, Segundo insists,

> Even the most enthusiastic defenders of "mass Christianity" cannot deny that there are two very different types of Christianity in Latin America. On the one hand, there is a majority Christianity of very low religious caliber, however much worth one may attribute to the people involved; on the other hand, there is a minority Christianity which is characterized by a much more profound grasp of the Christian message and the commitment it demands, however much one may accuse it of being class-conscious and intellectualistic. In other words, the difference itself is inescapable, no matter which kind one may feel inclined to prefer on the basis of a personal set of values.[63]

If Segundo's observations are undeniable, then the question arises whether a committed, elite vanguard of the Catholic masses are indeed the true subjects of liberation. Candelaria reads Segundo's response as affirmative: "For the Marxist branch of Liberation Theology, 'the people' are the working classes in conflict with the ruling classes," and popular culture and religion are considered "as 'primitive,' archaic, syncretistic, and alienating."[64]

However, a closer reading of Segundo reveals a more nuanced analysis. Segundo criticizes the view that "the Latin American masses are not only oppressed and exploited but also *alienated.* It is not just that they cannot express their own thoughts as liberated subjects of history. They cannot even think their own thoughts."[65] He avoids tying the majority-minority nexus to social class and instead locates it as an inherent dynamic within groups and individuals: "*Masses* and *minorities* are precisely what they are because they represent the two necessary poles of the economy of energy that rules the universe. They are the quantitative and qualitative poles present in any and every human group *but equally present in the patterns of conduct of each and every human individual.*"[66]

Segundo thereby escapes not only the simplistic identification of a particular social class as the subjects of liberation but also the risk of turning Christianity into what Weber considers a sect. Christianity is not constituted by "elitist religious groups who form their own closed circles, who possess their own distinctive beliefs and charismatic features, and who are not structured in terms of the roles and official positions that are part and parcel of the great religious traditions."[67] It is instead "supposed to be a leaven in the mass, a minority factor in itself,"[68] but "this does not point toward the maintenance of the interests of a small, self-enclosed group but rather toward the liberation of humanity—of the masses."[69]

For Segundo as well as for others representing general liberation theology, therefore, the subjects of liberation constitute this small group that acts as leaven for the liberation of the majority but are fully aware of the danger of falling into the alienated thinking of the majority.

Thus, the views of both currents of liberation theology on the subjects of liberation differ but only in their nuances. For both, "the people" remain the subjects of liberation. Though this refers to the nation for the Theology of the People, general liberation theology highlights the role of those within the population with an "enlightened consciousness." At the same time, the Theology of the People insists on the importance of evangelizing the people regarding the liberating force of the gospel.

Lived Christianity from the Liberationist Perspective

In contrast to the Vatican *Directory on Popular Piety* that sought to bring popular Christianity closer to official liturgy, the liberationist perspective links it with people's lives. This aligns it with McGuire's description of lived religion: "Rather than deduce an image of beliefs and practices from abstractions about religion in general or about particular religions, I have grappled with how to comprehend individuals' religions-as-practiced in all their complexity and dynamism."[70] Moreover, though it focuses on how "ordinary people [rather than official spokespersons]" live religion in their everyday lives, it is not merely subjective, as "people construct their religious worlds together, often sharing vivid experiences of their intersubjective reality."[71]

Both currents of the liberationist perspective link liberation to how people construct their communal and personal religious practice. This link is made more significant when the role that popular religion has played in many movements for social change and transformation is considered.

For instance, during Ferdinand Marcos's authoritarian regime (1972–86) in the Philippines, the Holy Week practice of the Stations of the Cross became a popular platform for social critique regarding their faith. Various local communities related issues such as land reform and militarization to various stages in Jesus's journey to Calvary. This practice echoed nineteenth-century movements in which, according to Ileto's historical study, "the masses' experience of Holy Week fundamentally shaped the style of peasant brotherhood and uprisings during the Spanish and early American colonial periods."[72]

However, this did not imply that those involved in such popular devotions consciously employed them in the name of liberation. As Ileto explains, what these popular practices provided lowland Philippine society was "a language for articulating its own values, ideals, and even hopes of liberation."[73]

This is also illustrated in Caroline Bynum's magisterial study of the place of food in the lives of holy medieval women. Texts from and about these women as well as their devotional practices related to food indicate not only their contribution in fostering eucharistic devotions but also, more importantly, how their words and actions transcended their traditional roles in church and society: "It is wrong to see medieval women as internalizing the idea of their gender as inferior."[74] Moreover,

> if it is inaccurate to see late medieval asceticism as self-hating because it is wrong to think that medieval people saw flesh primarily as opposed to spirit, it is doubly inaccurate to see female asceticism as based in dualism, because dualism was less important to women. Women saw themselves not as flesh opposed to spirit, female opposed to male, nurture opposed to authority; they saw themselves as human beings—fully spirit and fully flesh....Religious women in the later Middle Ages saw in their own female bodies not only a symbol of humanness of both genders but also a symbol of—and a means of approach to—the humanity of God.[75]

Thus, even though their religious practices did not set out to subvert traditional religious and gender roles, they were indeed liberating.

These historic and current illustrations of the place of popular religion in liberating practice provide a wider horizon for discussing the liberationist perspective on popular religion. As discussed in previous sections, both currents of the liberationist perspective view popular religion in relation to their location of the locus of liberation and their identification of its subjects.

Thus, general liberation theology and the Theology of the People examine whether and how popular practice promotes or hinders social transformation, and in so doing, they locate it at the core of these experiences. However, because of their different approaches to social analysis, they take different views of the link of popular Christianity to liberating practice as well as of the subjects of this practice.

General liberation theology, given its Marxist-inspired analysis, sees the practice and the adherents of popular Christianity as secondary to the change in the base economic structures of society. Though the practice of "enlightened" adherents could contribute to this transformation, popular Christianity is seen as promoting dualistic and fatalistic attitudes that domesticate adherents.

The premise for this negative view of popular Christianity appears to be what McGuire refers to as "overly cognitive approaches to individual religion."[76] General liberation theology considers the people's religion as alienating because it neither directly speaks against unjust social structures nor organizes people into concerted action.

This dominant emphasis on beliefs and attitudes recalls the Vatican *Directory*'s insistence that popular piety expresses theologically formulated doctrinal content. Moreover, as has been pointed out in the previous chapter, this emphasis overlooks the symbolic and narrative quality of popular Christianity, which is characterized by a practical rationality rather than by logical coherence.[77]

However, the Theology of the People sees the popular practice of the people as the significant expression of their faith in the context of their poverty, and thus as empowering them toward liberation. As Candelaria summarizes, "The values of popular Catholicism are being rediscovered because the Latin American people who are traditionally Catholic are recognized as the subjects of their own religiosity and agents of historical transformation"[78] and, because of its use of cultural analysis, "it is possible to trace an itinerary toward God using a hermeneutic of these symbols, myths, fiestas, rites, struggles, and utopias."[79] Thus popular Catholicism is accorded intrinsic value and does not just serve as an instrumental strategy for social transformation as general liberation theology holds.[80]

Notwithstanding this inherent valuation, the view of popular Catholicism within the liberationist perspective calls for further theological investigation. Greater reflection is needed to distinguish between the theological sense of "the people of God" and the meaning of "nation" or even "the nation-state," as well as between Christian salvation and historical liberation in the cultural, economic, and political realms. Scannone himself is not oblivious to this need, and thus emphasizes the importance of the evangelization of culture and discernment in Christian practice.

This need becomes more evident as Espín illustrates in his reflections on Our Lady of Guadalupe, the prime example in Latin American popular Catholicism.[81] His study opens an insightful path through the complex and multifaceted origin and reception of this much-studied devotion.

The origin of this devotion comes from a Marian apparition to the poor Amerindian Juan Diego in December 1531. His description of Mary echoes both Christian Marian iconography and Nahua imagery of the goddess Tonantzin. The apparition appeared at the hill of Tepeyac associated with Tonantzin. The Marian image bears native religious symbols associated with pregnancy and the power to reconcile opposites. The name Guadalupe is in fact a Spanish mispronunciation of *Tecoatlaxope*, an ancient Nahuatl term that means, "She will crush the serpent of stone." Despite these similarities, there are notable differences between the Christian and the native, the most important being the maternal tenderness of Our Lady of Guadalupe in contrast to the vindictive cruelty of the native goddess.

These similarities and differences in the religious iconography of Guadalupe noted in Juan Diego's personal vision need to be linked to its wider historical context. In Jeanette Rodriguez's reckoning, conquest, clash of cultures, and "subsequent devastation of an entire nation" provide the historical milieu for the apparition of Our Lady of Guadalupe.[82] This interplay between colonial missionary intent and native reception has shaped the devotion's significance throughout history. As Espín notes, "Precisely *because* Juan Diego claimed to have seen Mary *the way he did*, we can say today that this is a sign that the Christian gospel was in fact announced and accepted in early colonial Mexico, in spite of all the betrayals of the gospel that can be documented" and "was immediately judged to belong to the poor, since the educated and the wealthy had their Virgin of Remedios."[83]

Because of this intimate connection to the poor and indigenous people, the devotion has spread in and beyond colonial Mexico and has been recognized even by the official church. By 1564, its image arrived in colonial Philippines. Our Lady of Guadalupe became the patroness of Mexico City in 1737, and Pope Pius X declared Latin America under her patronage in 1910 and later included the Philippines in 1935. Though Pope Pius XII rescinded this in 1942, Pope John Paul II extended it to all the Americas by 1999.[84]

Furthermore, more fundamental than the official recognition is the ensuing vibrant tradition that has been embraced by and beyond those of Latino ancestry. A notable expression of this devotion are popular hymns and practices associated with Our Lady of Guadalupe, *Las Mañanitas*, an early morning serenade using traditional *ranchero* music with rewritten lyrics for Our Lady.

Both in its historical origins and its popular development, this devotion has been characterized by two aspects: "First of all, the Mary of Guadalupe has always been perceived by the poor as a tender mother, always compassionate, accepting, supportive, and forgiving. And secondly, she is seen as a protector, identified with her people, but most especially with the weakest and most in need. She procures justice for the oppressed and takes up their cause."[85]

This enduring legacy raises fundamental questions about the relationship of popular religion to the liberation of peoples, questions for which general liberation theology and even the Theology of the People do not sufficiently provide a theological basis. Though Our Lady of Guadalupe as a religious symbol does not directly promote liberation, its popular reception, especially among those poor and marginalized people, uncovers its liberating force—for instance, during the 1821 Mexican Revolution or the 1960s workers' protests led by Cesar Chavez and Dolores Huerta in the United States.

Given this, the theological status of devotions like Our Lady of Guadalupe needs to be articulated. Here, Espín criticizes two views often implicit in many Latin American reflections—that Our Lady of Guadalupe is either simply the same as or the "inculturated" image of the Mary of Scripture and Christian tradition. These views do not explain theologically "the depth of trust and affection that Latinos have for the *Virgen*" as well as "the beautiful, reverential relationship they nurture with her, and also how deeply touched and empowered they are by her," and thus, the theologian in Espín turns to what he refers to as "the extraordinary claims made for Guadalupe, the 'pneumatological' relationship implicated in the devotion, etc."[86] He elaborates what this relationship could entail by asking, "Don't we face a need to rethink the contents of these devotions in(to) pneumatological categories (i.e., *'vertir' las devociones y categorías supuestamente marianas, y sus contenidos, en categorías pneumatólogicas*), instead of continuing to insist on the Mary of Nazareth connection, in spite of this connection's apparent historical absence among everyday people?"[87] This leads to the following more particular questions: "Why can't we understand the 'Mary' categories in Latino Catholicism as *orthodox popular pneumatology*? Is there something inherent in the divine nature of the Spirit that prevents it from being imaged, spoken of, and related with in feminine categories?"[88] Such questions can be better addressed within the discussion of the theological status of lived religion in the next part.

PART III

SENSING THE PEOPLE'S FAITH

5

Lived Christianity and Christian Tradition

THOUGH UNDERSTANDING LIVED Christianity in terms of either worship or liberation highlights important dimensions of the people's faith, both perspectives prove to be incomplete for a theologically coherent and empirically informed account. The integral nature of lived Christianity is better understood within Christian tradition, both its dynamics as well as its content.[1] When described by the *Catechism of the Catholic Church* as that which "comes from the apostles and hands on what they received from Jesus' teaching and example and what they learned from the Holy Spirit," tradition is often rendered with a capital *T*.[2] In contrast, "traditions" refers to particular examples of what is transmitted with varying degrees of normativity.

This chapter does not offer a general theology of tradition but an understanding of tradition that explicitly provides a significant place for lived Christianity. It draws insights from contemporary theological reflection on tradition, generated in part by increased awareness of contextual diversity and religious plurality. It employs insights from the earlier groundbreaking works of Congar and the more recent *Tradition: Understanding Christian Tradition* by Gerald O'Collins[3] and brings their perspective in relation to lived Christianity. The chapter first proposes that lived Christianity—how Christian individuals and groups practice their religion—is integral to Christian tradition, and then discusses various themes related to tradition in this context. In referencing instances of how Christians live their faith in daily life, such a discussion not only enfleshes a theology of tradition but also brings into focus the sense and significance of lived Christianity.

Lived Christianity's Place in Christian Tradition

In line with contemporary theological reflection on Christian tradition, O'Collins highlights two important features: its fundamental basis in God's revelation and, therefore, its inclusive character.

First, O'Collins underscores the essential link between tradition and revelation and thus recasts the historic and commonly perceived opposition between Scripture and tradition. This opposition has been part of the historical baggage from what McGuire refers to as the "Long Reformation," when "both Catholic and Protestant churches experienced a series of change-promoting movements that aimed to reform Christianity. These reformations were about literally re-forming, re-shaping, and re-defining the core of Christian faith and practice."[4] Protestants were seen as dismissing tradition in favor of *sola scriptura*, while Catholics were seen as defending the essential significance of tradition, especially its doctrinal content.

Given the temporal distance from these conflicts and the close reading of historical and contemporary Catholic and Protestant documents, recent theological reflection helps overcome the binary opposition between Scripture and tradition. To this end, O'Collins compares the 1963 report "Tradition and Traditions" from the Protestant *Faith and Order Conference* in Montreal[5] with the Second Vatican Council's Dogmatic Constitution *Dei Verbum* of 1965 and finds that both texts "suggest convergent lines of thinking and so provide a background toward discussing today the nature and role of tradition for Christians."[6]

Both documents highlight the central view that "revelation is *primarily* a personal encounter with God (who is Truth) rather than the communication of a body of hitherto unknown truths."[7] This shared view describes revelation as the fundamental process of God's self-disclosure in Christ through the history of salvation and thus provides the foundation for understanding the revelatory character of tradition. The Montreal Report could not have been more emphatic when it describes tradition as *Christus praesens*: "The Tradition of the Church is not an object which we *possess* but a reality by which we are *possessed*."[8]

This view of revelation provides the horizon for connecting tradition and Scripture: "Testimony to the divine self-revelation on the part of the Old Testament prophets (understood in the broad sense) and the New Testament apostles (likewise understood in the broad sense) inaugurated the tradition."[9] The structure of *Dei Verbum* reflects this central link between revelation (chapter 1), tradition (chapter 2), and Scripture (chapter 3). This link is also echoed by the Montreal Report: "The oral and written tradition of the prophets and the apostles under the guidance of the Holy Spirit led to the formation of Scripture and to the canonization of the Old and New Testaments as the Bible of the Church."[10]

Differences between Catholic and Protestant perspectives on tradition regarding the nature of doctrinal development or the status of infallible definitions remain.[11] However, both perspectives converge in the fundamental link of Scripture and tradition to God's self-disclosure.

Second, since tradition mediates God's revelation intended for all, its scope cannot but be inclusive. As O'Collins underscores, both documents "embodied 'total' views of tradition as being the whole *living heritage* which is passed on."[12] *Dei Verbum* declares, "What was handed on by the Apostles includes everything that contributes to making the People of God live their life in holiness and grow in faith. In this way, the Church, in her doctrine, life and worship, perpetuates and transmits to all generations everything that she herself is, everything that she believes" (*Dei Verbum* 9).[13] In a similar vein, the Montreal Report states, "What is transmitted in the process of tradition is the Christian faith, not only as a sum of tenets (equivalent to 'everything that she [the Church] believes' of DV 8) but [also] as a living reality transmitted through the operations of the Holy Spirit."[14]

This inclusive view of tradition and its foundation in revelation as divine self-disclosure indicates the integral place of lived Christianity within tradition. How Christians live their faith in everyday life rightly belongs to Christian tradition.

However, official and theological discussions of Christian tradition have often been restricted to the spheres of doctrine, liturgy, and theology. For instance, the *Directory on Popular Piety* discussed in chapter 3 merely describes popular piety, which is "characterized by a great variety and richness of bodily, gestural and symbolic expressions" (no. 15), as "part of popular tradition" (no. 17). In its few references to the tradition of the church, its primary focus lies in what church tradition states regarding particular beliefs or practices; for instance, that the veneration of images of the saints is defended by the Council of Nicaea "following the divinely inspired teaching of our Holy Fathers and the tradition of the Catholic Church" (no. 238). All this despite its own declaration that popular piety is "a true treasure of the people of God" and "a living reality in and of the Church" with "the constant presence of the Spirit of God in the ecclesial community" as its source (no. 61).

If indeed popular piety is a true treasure of the people of God whose source is the constant presence of the Holy Spirit, lived Christianity—"how religion and spirituality are practiced, experienced, and expressed by ordinary people (rather than official spokespersons) in the context of their everyday lives"[15]—is an integral part of Christian tradition. After all, "what was handed on by the Apostles includes *everything* that contributes to making the People of God live their lives in holiness and grow in faith" (*Dei Verbum* 9).

No wonder that O'Collins discusses a wide range of "examples taken from Christian tradition": among them, "baptism, creeds, the Eucharist, marriage symbols, the Prayers of the Faithful, the RCIA, ashes, palms, music, incense, holy water, candles...."[16] Moreover, he emphasizes that "we should not forget the multitude of lay Christians who have inherited and contributed to *traditions of caring* for the sick and elderly, helping the poor, teaching children and serving others in many social ministries....Particular traditions of Christian service, along with institutional forms of religious life, reveal and transmit the reality of *Christus praesens*, the *Traditum* at the heart of all Christian living and serving."[17]

All these forms in and through which individuals and groups live Christianity constitute the very fabric of lived Christianity as an integral part of tradition. Though these manifold forms may not have equal value or uniform coherence, *Unitatis Redintegratio* states, "This whole heritage (*patrimonium*) of spirituality and liturgy, of discipline and theology, in its various traditions belongs to the full catholicity and apostolicity of the Church."[18]

Moreover, as part of Christian tradition, lived Christianity shares in the revelatory character of tradition insofar as it consists of people's response in faith to God's self-disclosure in and through the Body of Christ and its members. This faith response to revelation transmitted by the process of tradition is inseparable from God's enduring self-disclosure in the history of salvation. As Robert Schreiter notes, "The gospel is always incarnate, incarnate in the reality of those who bring it to us, and incarnate in those who help us nurture the beginnings of faith. Church is the complex of those cultural patterns in which the gospel has taken on flesh."[19]

This incarnation provides the fundamental ground for the integral and inclusive relation between lived Christianity and Christian tradition. Hispanic theologian Orlando Espín highlights the Spanish expression *lo cotidiano* as "the real life that is lived, lived and experienced by real people, in the everyday"[20]—where "the People of God, individually and communally, have experienced revelation and encountered God."[21] Within "the one existential space and ever-present moment in which God reveals Godself and humans respond in faith (or not),"[22] those who follow Jesus constitute "the People of God who *are* the Church and, therefore, who are of paramount protagonic importance. It is *their* faith and real faith-life, therefore, and *their* traditioning."[23]

Agency in Tradition and Christian Identity

Locating lived Christianity within Christian tradition brings into focus the important theme of agency or, in technical theological language, the subject of tradition and its relation to Christian identity. This theme raises the question regarding who the driving force in the emergence, preservation, and transmission of tradition is.

In his classic study of tradition, Congar distinguishes between the transcendental and historical subjects of Christian tradition. The first he identifies as the Holy Spirit, "the bond of love between the Father and the Son [who] is also the strong link between God and his external activity in establishing a fellowship between himself and mankind."[24] In this unfolding of divine self-revelation, the Holy Spirit "animates the apostles and the Church from within, to enable them to carry out the work with which they are entrusted."[25]

In animating apostolic witness, this Spirit of Christ "realizes and gives depth to *what* was said and done once and for all by Christ, which is the Gospel."[26] Given this, Christian tradition, which is none other than "the transmission of the Gospel in and through the Church from Christ and the apostles," has the Holy Spirit as "its most profound and definite, though 'transhistorical,' subject."[27] As a transcendent subject of tradition, therefore, the Holy Spirit preserves God's revelation in Christ and ensures its faithful transmission.

This animating work of the Holy Spirit, however, unfolds within history, and the church as the community of disciples receives and transmits the gospel as the historical subject of tradition. As a passive subject, the church receives God's revelation in Christ through the apostolic witness but, as an active subject, also transmits this witness to succeeding generations of Christians.

In animating the missionary witness of the church, this same Spirit "ensure[s] from within that many different people down the centuries and scattered over the surface of the globe share in this unique form of truth and life"[28] and "promotes a fellowship of all the members with one another in the same truth."[29] The Spirit is truly "the profound and transcendent principle of *identity*, since unchanging and unique, he is the Church's operative principle."[30]

This activity of ecclesial witness belongs to the entire church—the baptized—and is indeed the historical subject of Christian tradition. Congar notes that, in accordance with the nature of revelation and tradition, "all the members of the Body of Christ are alive and living, active and responsible" and "*all* men have a responsibility, on the basis of their mere life itself, to share, bear witness and to serve."[31]

This all-encompassing nature of the church as a historical subject of Christian tradition is the fundamental basis for situating the differing roles of official and unofficial witnesses. As Congar notes, "The laity's dependence on the hierarchical magisterium for the receiving of the objective determinations of the faith does not prevent the faithful from being a subject, which is irreducible to the magisterium, or, as is frequently said (since when?), to the teaching Church."[32]

Along the same lines, O'Collins insists that "we should not neglect the *unofficial* transmitters of tradition. They cannot establish themselves as transmitters of tradition by producing such official documents as certificates of ordination, marriage, or appointment to theological faculties. But while official transmitters can fail in their tasks, gifted, unofficial individuals, by the test of time, established themselves as hugely influential in passing on the Christian tradition."[33] Moreover, though "the acts which the faithful perform as a corporate subject of tradition consists principally in its preservation and transmission," they transmit it "by teaching and education" and "by witnessing to and professing the faith."[34] Their entire life, then, expresses their role as true historical subjects of tradition, "whether because it *effectively* transmits the Gospel, and hence enters 'active tradition,' or because it constitutes a genuine *locus theologicus*, entering thus into the general assemblage of witnesses, signs, or monuments of Tradition."[35]

Given this, lived Christianity's emphasis on personal and communal agency aligns with this theological description of the entire church as a historical subject of Christian tradition. In stressing how individuals and groups live Christianity in their everyday experience, it underscores their role, first, as passive subjects standing within the tradition they belong to and receiving God's revelation in the apostolic and ecclesial witness, and second, as active subjects appropriating this tradition in living Christianity and passing it on to others.

This theological account of the whole church as a historical subject of tradition becomes incarnated through how Christians as the Body of Christ exercise their agency. Here, *agency* refers to the whole range of concrete action and behavior undertaken by Christians in living their faith rather than to the narrow technical meaning as freedom from limitation, interference, or domination.[36] In particular, it refers to how they shape their identity as disciples "in the world but not of it."

With the Spirit of Christ as "the profound and transcendent principle of *identity*," the corporate people of God, as well as all the baptized, share in this identity of Christian discipleship.[37] Moreover, the scope of this shared identity includes those distant from the institutional centers of church community for various pastoral reasons: the poor, for instance, with no easy access to parishes, or the divorced or remarried Catholics separated from ordinary church life. Many among them strive to live a life of discipleship.

Christian identity is far from being a static characteristic attributed to the church as an organic entity and to individual members, but is truly a dynamic process of becoming rather than being that "help[s] Christianity expand its horizons of self-understanding and grow toward greater truth."[38] Within this ecclesial process, individual Christians exercise agency, "constantly *on their way toward* deeper participation in their identity as Christians."[39] Thus, there is a convergence of God's ongoing work in creation and human history, on the one hand, and our personal and collective stories, on the other, that therefore creates identity "in the narrative crossover, in the cross over from one to the other."[40] Consequently, both the church and individual Christians shape their Christian identity, drawing from the rich diversity of everyday life and appropriate elements from resources within Christian religious practice, their social and cultural locations, and other traditions, religious or otherwise. Just as Terence Tilley states that religious tradition is not entirely "made or given,"[41] Christian identity is shaped neither as a static essence nor as a pure construction.[42]

Church history offers countless illustrations of how Christianity borrowed elements from its surrounding milieu for its doctrinal formulations and sacramental practices, among others. One of O'Collins's examples mentions "the adoption of symbols previously used in civil ceremonies and then incorporated permanently into the liturgy for Christian marriage: for instance, the veil worn by the bride, her ring, and her joining hands with the bridegroom. Such traditional details have not unraveled with the passage of time, but have been preserved because they help sustain the identity of Christian marriage and its connection with Christ himself."[43] In seventeenth-century Philippines, the chosen word for the sacrament of baptism was Tagalog *binyag* rather than the Spanish *bautismo*, which referred to Muslim rites of purification.[44]

With the great volume and variety of social and religious resources accessible in the contemporary global situation, Christian identity "hinges on remaining open to direction from the free grace of God" and, at the same time, is unavoidably multilayered, relating to all other layers of communal and personal identification such as ethnicity, gender, or class.[45]

This interplay has led the sociologist J. N. Pieterse and theologian Robert Schreiter, among others, to speak of identity in terms of hybridity.[46] This, however, neither implies what used to be pejoratively called "syncretism," meaning the unintegrated juxtaposition of disparate elements, nor the reduction of Christian identity to other identifications such as class ideology. Such reduction betrays Christian identity, as Michael Budde illustrates with the identification of capitalist interests with Christianity within American society.[47]

This hybrid character of Christian identity has brought up the issue regarding the possibility of multiple religious belonging. Though some have understood this as some form of "cafeteria Christianity" as could be implied in Cornille's view,[48] others, especially those such as Laksana writing within Asian contexts, prefer to acknowledge the complexity of religious belonging.[49] Describing Christian identity as hybrid clearly highlights its interaction with other identifications (as opposed to the European understanding of religion as a comprehensive system of beliefs, ethical norms, and religious practices), as living Christianity is not isolated from but profoundly engaged in all the dimensions of everyday life.[50]

Ari Dy's religious ethnography of the Chinese in the Philippines offers an example.[51] This sector shapes their religious identity through the interaction of different layers of their concrete lives: Chinese and Filipino in terms of ethnic culture; and Buddhist and Christian in terms of religious tradition. Those with stronger links to Chinese tradition, such as first-generation immigrants from China, identify themselves as Chinese with some Filipino influences, whereas those Philippine-born identify more as Chinese Filipinos (*Tsinoys*). This dynamic also applies to their religious identity. Some consider themselves to be primarily Buddhist, steeped in Buddhist tradition and described by Dy as "the elite," while others identify themselves as Christians engaged in Buddhist practices.

In Dy's analysis, the articulation of religious identity is based on what is substantive (the nominative) and what is the modifier (the adjective). Some identify themselves as Buddhist but qualified as *Tsinoys* with Christian influences; others as Christian but qualified as *Tsinoys* with Buddhist influences. Both groups participate in the social development work of the Taiwan-based Tzu Chi foundation, as shown in their extensive work among all victims of the 2016 Super Typhoon Haiyan, providing food and shelter as well as rebuilding their churches and mosques. Those among them identifying as Christian exercise their agency as subjects of Christian tradition and consider such participation integral to living Christianity.

Through their action and behavior, Christians forge their identity in their everyday life and contribute to the articulation of the common identity of the Body of Christ as disciples and historical subjects of Christian tradition.

Faithful Traditioning, Changing Traditions

The historical subject of Christian tradition—the church as Body of Christ and its members—exercise their agency in relation to both the process and content of tradition. Like all other traditions, Christian tradition consists of the process of transmission as well as the content that is transmitted.

This dual reference is of great significance for understanding Christian tradition, which involves transmission of God's self-disclosure in history through Christ as well as changes in particular traditions during this process. In effect, the relation between faithful transmission and changing traditions interrogates the nature of our relation to the process of tradition itself and the possibility of changing traditions within this relation. Formulated as a straightforward question, it inquires whether our location within the process of faithful transmission curtails the possibility of changing specific contents of tradition, especially those perceived as ideological.

Here, insights from the Gadamer-Habermas debate, each representing hermeneutics and ideology-critique respectively, and Ricoeur's commentary prove helpful.[52] Ricoeur points to the central issue beneath this complex technical debate: "Is it possible to formulate a hermeneutics which would render justice to the critique of ideology?"[53]

Gadamer's *Truth and Method* proposes an understanding of tradition (*Überlieferung*) different from the Enlightenment view of tradition as contrary to reason and thus bereft of any validity and authority. Drawing from his analysis of aesthetics, history, and language, he describes our relation to tradition, which "is not simply a process that we learn to know and be in command of through experience; it is language, i.e., it expresses itself like a 'Thou.' A 'Thou' is not an object, but it stands in a relationship with us."[54] Thus, "to stand within a tradition does not limit the freedom of knowledge but makes it possible."[55]

This insight from Gadamer is echoed by contemporary theologians of Christian tradition. O'Collins explicitly references Gadamer when he writes, "Tradition is 'the way we relate to the past' or the way the past is present. Hence 'we are always situated within a tradition'; 'tradition is always part of us.'"[56] Our being situated within the process of Christian tradition, or "traditioning" as Dale Irvin prefers, is not only "the process of handing on the faith to a next generation" but also "a 'passing over,' as well as the Christian movement has crossed religious and cultural boundaries in mission."[57] Thus, "traditions provide a sense of stability, a community space in which people can dwell, and a set of practices that shape how the participants live in the world, even though many participants who dwell in those traditions realize that they have evolved from what they were when they were founded."[58]

Belonging to or standing within tradition, therefore, does not militate against but in fact facilitates change, as the process of "passing on" to succeeding generations engages elements from new and diverse contexts. For Christian tradition, this process is guided by the activity of the Holy Spirit as a transcendent subject of tradition. As Congar writes, there is "no 'incarnation' of the Holy Spirit in the Church like the Incarnation of the Word of God in Jesus Christ; there is simply a Covenant between them, guaranteed by God's absolute fidelity."[59]

Moreover, this understanding of tradition as fundamental ground, Gadamer insists, does not compromise the autonomy of will and the faculty of reason of the individual person.[60]

Thus, Gadamer rehabilitates the pejorative concept of prejudice as contrary to reason and imposed from external authority. As the fundamental ground upon which we stand, traditioning incorporates prejudice, which "means a judgement is given before all the elements that determine a situation have all been examined," but this "certainly does not mean a false judgment but it is part of the idea that it can have a positive and a negative value."[61] This makes possible the examination of particular elements of tradition or specific traditions through what he refers to as *wirkunggesichtliches Bewusstsein*, which Ricoeur translates as "consciousness exposed to the effects of history" or "consciousness of historical efficacy."[62] Against this view, Habermas brings out his fundamental objection to Gadamer's hermeneutics, which does not in itself guarantee "that there are legitimate prejudices."[63] Furthermore, this hermeneutics, which builds on the linguistic character of tradition, becomes suspect because "language is also a medium of domination and social power; it serves to legitimate relations of organized force."[64] Habermas insists that "here it is a question not of deceptions within a language but of deception with language as such."[65]

Given this, the critique of ideological contents of tradition requires recognizing that "*social actions can only be comprehended in an objective framework that is constituted conjointly by language, labor and domination.*"[66] This objective framework lies in Ricoeur's theory of communicative action, which sets up the conditions for an ideal speech situation devoid of any ideological forces.[67]

Ricoeur's commentary on this debate, while respecting their stark differences about the fundamental gesture and ground of philosophy, shows "that each can recognize the other's claim to universality in a way which marks the place of one in the structure of the other."[68]

Employing his analysis of related dialectics between appropriation and dissociation, between explanation and understanding, and between sense and reference developed in his *Interpretation Theory*,[69] he suggests that "the two 'universals,' that of hermeneutics and that of the critique of ideology are interpenetrating."[70] Moreover, "the two claims cross on a common ground: the hermeneutics of finitude, which secures *a priori* the correlation between the concept of prejudice and that of reason."[71]

Hence, based on this common ground, a critical hermeneutics affirms "that man can project his emancipation only on the basis of the creative reinterpretation of cultural heritage"[72] and that this reinterpretation includes changing ideological elements of this heritage. In the end, Ricoeur calls attention to the fact that "critique is also a tradition. I would even say that it plunges into the most impressive tradition, that of liberating acts, of the Exodus and the Resurrection."[73]

These insights from the debate between hermeneutics and ideology-critique affirm that recognizing our grounding in Christian traditioning does not hinder us from changing particular traditions. Historical studies point to countless examples of this dynamic in every area of Christian life. Aside from doctrinal formulations that often preoccupy studies on tradition, many other aspects of Christian life, such as sacramental rites and religious practices, have emerged through the concrete interaction between elements of Christian heritage and concrete situations of the church. Thus, the church has remained faithful in its traditioning while changing some traditions. In other words, catholicity and contextuality are not separate from and opposed to each other. To borrow the words of the church in Asia, "inculturation is not mere adaptation of a ready-made Christianity into a given situation, but rather a creative embodiment of the Word in the local church."[74] This continuing and eschatological dialogue is embodied in how the Body of Christ and its members live their faith in their contexts, faithfully passing on and passing over the boundless mystery of God's presence in the world.

Change in the Content of Christian Traditioning

Given that Christian traditioning inherently involves change—either due to interaction with new contexts or because of traditions that have become ideological in nature—there arises the question of whether there is unchanging content in tradition.

This unchanging content is associated among Protestants with the gospel of Jesus Christ and among Catholics with "the deposit of faith." Despite the differences in the vocabulary and in what each identifies as unchanging, both views share the conviction of an unchanging content because of what God has revealed for the salvation of all. Though this section focuses on the Catholic discussion about the deposit of faith, its exploration applies to what is indeed unchanging for all Christians and what this implies for Christian life and reflection.

The phrase *the deposit of faith* has been explicitly associated in Catholic teaching with the unchanging content of tradition. This nomenclature is originally drawn from the Latin Vulgate translation of the New Testament *parathēkē* and intended to refer to "all that God revealed through Christ for human salvation" and "a treasure entrusted to the Church to be preserved and handed on faithfully to all people until the end of time."[75] This phrase has endured in subsequent theological reflection and official church documents.

For instance, O'Collins points out that Vatican II documents use this nomenclature in the following references: *Lumen Gentium* 25; *Unitatis Redintegratio* 6; *Dei Verbum* 10; and *Gaudium et Spes* 62. Similar references speak of "the deposit of the Word of God" (*Gaudium et Spes* 33),[76] "the deposit of Revelation" (*Lumen Gentium* 25), and "the treasure of Revelation" (*Dei Verbum* 26). All these instances rightly link the deposit of faith to God's revelation memorialized in Scripture and tradition.

However, O'Collins also points out that the word *deposit*, in ancient as well as contemporary usage, commonly refers to objects and, when applied to God's self-disclosure, could give rise to ambiguity. Even

Flannery's translation in *Dei Verbum*—"the things he had revealed" (no. 7) and "things revealed" (no. 9)—carry this connotation of the deposit as object-like, whereas the Vatican's official translation reads "what He had revealed" (*Quae Deus ad salutem cunctarum gentium revelaverat*) and "everything which has been revealed" (*de omnibus revelatis*). Aside from this linguistic connotation, the deposit of faith or whatever is considered the unchanging basis of Christianity is memorialized in and tied to normative texts, whether Scripture alone or, for Catholics, together with authoritative magisterial teaching. Even those called by Congar "monuments or witnesses of tradition" are similarly textual.[77] These monuments—the church's liturgy, the fathers of the church, and official doctrinal statements—are "not tradition itself, which transcends them; they are the concrete expression of various aspects of it and thus, for us, a means of reaching this tradition and identifying it."[78]

Hence, everything linked to the unchanging content of God's self-disclosure in both Scripture and tradition are fundamentally textual. Moreover, the object-like appearance of all these texts reinforces views that the unchanging content of Christianity is also object-like, like those found in forms of biblical and doctrinal fundamentalism.

But such textual objects are mute in themselves. Thus, Congar elaborates the role of normative texts: "The text controls it, but tradition clarifies the text, which is no more than a witness of facts and realities by which the Church lives and that she possesses. The *deposit* is richer than its written expression."[79] What Congar draws from this textuality regarding tradition applies to Scripture and its relation to tradition: "It is true that what flows afresh in the transmitting channel comes entirely from *the* original and unique source, which we know to be Jesus Christ and his saving Gospel....But this source is not restricted to the content of a text; it is an ever-active reality, alive in the Church. The deposit in its primitive documentary form is not the sole principle responsible for the value of what has been communicated two, ten or twenty centuries later."[80] Profound questions from succeeding generations "[demand] answers from the Gospel, whose deposit is carried by the Church as a holy ark upon a turbulent sea....If God, having said all that he had to tell us in Jesus Christ, no longer intervenes in the world by a new public Revelation, he expects to see his People giving forth the Word it has received, once again—a thousand times again—for the healing of the nation (cf. Rev 22:2)."[81]

Thus, while God's self-disclosure in Christ memorialized in Scripture and transmitted faithfully by the Body of Christ and its members remains definitive and unchanging, its meaning is elaborated through the church's life and mission in the unfolding of history and the encounter with new contexts. The salvific Word of God in Jesus Christ is ever made afresh in the preaching and witness of Christian discipleship and therefore is elaborated in and through the process of traditioning with varying degrees of authority. Thus, while the integrity of the deposit of faith is preserved, it undergoes development, not only in doctrine but also in all elements of tradition.[82]

Moreover, this integral task of elaborating the deposit of faith does not only apply to normative texts but also to the nontextual elements of tradition such as sacramental and other spiritual practices. Throughout its history, the church has explicated the meaning of these practices for Christian life and mission. Moreover, theological and pastoral reflection have even ventured into articulating the essence of Christianity because of various doctrinal and contextual considerations.[83] Though legitimate and even necessary, such articulations are never easily arrived at, universally uncontested, or definitively closed to further elaboration, given the faithful guidance of the Holy Spirit in the unfolding of God's self-disclosure in history.

This relation between the text and its elaboration is affirmed by Ricoeur's textual hermeneutics. In his analysis, though a text originates from an author to an intended audience within a particular context, this text as text is not tied to its original circumstances and thus assumes an autonomy that opens it up to readers in different contexts. This autonomy from the author "results from the disconnection of the mental intention of the author from the verbal meaning of the text, of what the author meant and what the text means."[84] At the same time, textual autonomy from the original intended audience becomes accessible to "an indefinite number of readers and, therefore, of interpretations," hence the ongoing task of interpreting Scripture and the texts of tradition.[85]

Moreover, Ricoeur considers this dissociation from author and audience as productive. He does not disregard the importance of examining the text's original circumstances and affirms the importance of historical-critical studies of the text and puts it under the rubric of explaining (*erklären*) the world behind the text. However, he insists that understanding the text is not restricted to what these exegetical studies arrive at. On the contrary, "the sense of a text is not behind the text but in front of it. It is not something hidden, but something disclosed. What has to be understood is not the initial situation of discourse, but what points toward a possible world, thanks to the non-ostensive reference of the text. Understanding has less than ever to do with the author and his situation. It seeks to grasp the world-propositions opened up by the reference of the text. To understand the text is to follow its movement from sense to reference, from what it says, to what it talks about."[86]

Paraphrased in relation to Christianity, to understand the meaning of "the revelatory text"[87] of the deposit of faith is to grasp the eschatological reign of God proclaimed by Christ. When read by the Body of Christ and its members, this mute but authoritative text is transformed into a voice that opens new horizons when read by new interlocutors in new contexts. As succeeding generations of disciples of Christ, Christians read the revelatory text and hear God's Word as a contemporary event. The deposit of faith endures, but its elaboration by and in the Body of Christ gives rise to an abundance of meaning.

Explicating the integral place of lived Christianity within Christian tradition highlights the inclusive and dynamic nature of Christian tradition. The corporate Body of Christ and all its members exercise their agency as a historical subject of tradition by receiving in faith and transmitting God's revelation to others. This process of Christian tradition encompasses the concrete and specific ways in which all Christians live their faith and forge their identity as disciples in their everyday life and contexts. By living Christianity, what they strive to receive and transmit consists of nothing less than the deposit of faith constantly vibrant and contemporary. Such a perspective on lived Christianity in the context of Christian tradition finds its most visible expression in Pope Francis's religious practice and reflection on popular piety. Known for religious devotions to Sleeping Saint Joseph and Our Lady the Undoer of Knots, among others, he has pointed to the theological and pastoral significance of popular piety in his first apostolic exhortation, *Evangelii Gaudium*: "Each portion of the people of God, by translating the gift of God into its own life and in accordance with its own genius, bears witness to the faith it has received and enriches it with new and eloquent expressions....Herein lies the importance of popular piety, a true expression of the spontaneous missionary activity of the people of God. This is an ongoing and developing process, of which the Holy Spirit is the principal agent" (no. 122).[88]

Moreover, when the church fails to recognize that "popular piety, as a fruit of the inculturated Gospel, is an active evangelizing power," then it "would be to fail to recognize the work of the Holy Spirit" (no. 126).

6

A Theological Exploration of Marian Practice

THE PRECEDING CHAPTER offered a theological account of the place of lived Christianity within Christian tradition. This chapter focuses on the theological status of religious practices of Christian groups and individuals in the context of their ordinary lives. We explore how lived Christianity in Christian tradition could deepen our understanding of the theological sense and sociological significance of these practices.

To illustrate the place of lived Christianity within Christian tradition, we consider the general phenomenon of practices generally associated with Mary. Besides being perhaps the most visible in Christian tradition and often an important part of how Christians live their faith, these devotions clearly embody the general characteristics of similar religious practices that are part of Christian tradition and are associated with exemplary personages, whether biblical or not. Like the apostles James in Spain and Thomas in India, St. Isidore the Farmer, patron of farmers, and St. Rita of Cascia, patron of hopeless cases, these devotional practices, including those of Mary, bear an explicit or implicit claim of a transcendent character, expressed in word and action—with some involving apparitions, auditions, or venerated objects. They are accorded some degree of popularity and recognition from the faithful and church offices that could be enduring or short-lived.

Even in relation to Jesus Christ, God's definitive self-disclosure and Christianity's central figure, associated religious practices focusing on certain life events and doctrinal titles have emerged and developed along the same lines as these other devotional practices. For instance, the development of the Philippine devotion to the *Santo Niño de Cebu* (Holy Child of Cebu) reflects the unfolding of Christian evangelization and native reception of the faith and has been regarded as key to "figuring Catholicism" in Philippine contemporary life.[1] According to historical accounts, the image of the Child Jesus came with the first Spanish expedition in 1521, inaugurating five hundred years of Christianity in the nation. The image—one of an approximately five-year-old with bejeweled crown and cape and with one hand holding a globe and the other in blessing—remains present in the lives of countless devotees in and beyond Cebu. Its varying reproductions appear in churches, homes, and vehicles, as well as in unusual garb such as police, fisherman, and other occupations of devotees. Given his study's intertwined aims of figuring out the place of the material image in devotional practice as well as the recurring discourses about the Santo Niño, Bautista notes, "The Santo Niño is today accorded the same degree of reverence as a priceless national treasure or an irreplaceable historical artifact.... What most Filipinos agree upon is that the Santo Niño, or the Niño for short, stands as a tangible representation of Filipinos' Catholic identity, such that its survival is itself a metaphor for how the faithful have fared amidst the many tribulations in their tumultuous history."[2]

Analogous insights are echoed and analyzed in this chapter on Marian devotion, which finds expression in countless practices.[3] Many examples of Marian devotion are attached to church celebrations such as Christmas and Holy Week; religious groups such as the Dominicans' Our Lady of the Most Holy Rosary and the Jesuits' *Maria della Strada* (Our Lady of the Way); particular places such as the apparition in the 1530s at Tepeyac, Mexico, and in 1917 at Fatima, Portugal; and specific needs addressed to Our Lady of Perpetual Help and Our Lady, Undoer of Knots, a Pope Francis favorite. Though this phenomenon is especially present in but not limited to Catholic practice, some from different Christian and other traditions have been known to take part in these practices as well.[4]

The ubiquity and diversity of these practices make this phenomenon exceedingly complex. At different times and places, representations of

Mary's figure have stressed different traits, including virgin, mother, exemplar, or disciple. This complex phenomenon has attracted vibrant scholarly attention, initially from church-related fields such as biblical studies, theology, and spirituality, but more recently from multiple disciplines and combinations thereof, such as anthropology, psychology, and sociology. These studies, especially the interdisciplinary ones, note similarities and differences in many Marian practices. For instance, some scholars focus on Mary's figure in relation to "the feminine" in various historical contexts.[5] And yet she is considered either as the quintessential representation of docility or the herald of personal agency and transformation in a patriarchal social and religious culture.[6] Others characterize Marian devotions as symbolic expressions within situations of societal stress and conflict.[7]

Though these and other similar characterizations prescind from the strictly theological nature of Marian devotion because of their disciplinal perspectives, they nevertheless offer enriching insights for a theological account of Marian devotion within Christian tradition.

This chapter does not directly engage specific issues from these studies but draws insights from representative studies for its sketch of the theological dynamic in Marian devotional practice. Its specific aim is to explore this dynamic in terms of the interplay between transhistorical and local impulses behind this phenomenon. On the one hand, these devotions have traveled across changing historical periods. On the other hand, they have taken root and been transformed in diverse locations. Though these impulses are inherent and thus present in each devotional practice, either of them has proven to be dominant through changing times and spaces. The following theological exploration of this interplay helps articulate the incarnate sense and significance of lived Christianity.

Moving across Historical Times and Places

The transhistorical impulse behind these practices is occasioned by the sparse biblical references to Mary. Given the New Testament's christocentric message, Mary's figure, though important in the life and ministry of Jesus, is mentioned only in relation to Jesus's birth and childhood, some instances during his ministry, and his passion and death. Hence, subsequent traditions from the early church onward filled in gaps in her life story, established various venerable titles and devotions, and further articulated authoritative theological implications of the biblical witness.

In relation to this historical development, the genealogy of the words *Marian* and *Marianism* is instructive. According to De la Cruz, these terms initially appeared in different contexts—the first as a defensive apologetic during the Protestant Reformation, and the second as a nineteenth-century Enlightenment indictment against Christianity itself. But both signify "the novel abstraction of categories from the figure of Mary, Mother of God."[8] Such a linguistic conceptualization, far from diminishing the role of Mary, paves the way for its transhistoricalization. No longer restricted to the sparse biblical texts, Mary's figure has acquired a wider reach and becomes more accessible.

This accessibility further underscores the transhistorical quality of Marian devotion. According to De la Cruz, the neologism *Marian* suggests "a transcendent figure with a singular identity" and "prioritizes the universal and general over the local and particular."[9]

Hence, wide proliferation of Marian devotional practices historically coincided with the emergence of this conceptual vocabulary. For instance, during the long Reformation that shaped both doctrinal beliefs and religious practices among Catholics and Protestants alike, Mary's figure not only became "the acknowledged defender of the Catholic Church against the Protestant movement in the sixteenth century";[10] rather, the growing stress on spiritual interiority in Catholic circles, partly but not exclusively due to Protestantism, further led to greater emphasis on Mary's spiritual motherhood and not just her bodily connection with Jesus: "Before Mary was able to conceive Christ bodily, she had become his spiritual mother through faith and the willingness to do God's will"[11] and turned into "a role model, someone whose piety and receptivity to God's word could be imitated by all Christians."[12]

Therefore, although "bodily present in heaven, Mary was still accessible to the faithful through her many images and relics, scattered throughout Europe, and could be counted on to show mercy to any who sought her aid."[13] With this dispersal throughout Europe during the fifteenth and sixteenth centuries, "Marian devotion blossomed as a major part of a religious culture" and became "in essence the result of an active dialogue between, on the one hand, the religion of the laity, manifested in miracle stories, popular rituals, commissioned art, and plays, and, on the other, the existing structure of the liturgy and formal ecclesiastical teaching in which medieval piety also found expression."[14]

With this dispersal in different places came the impulse toward localization. Mary's figure took on differing nuances—for example, in the "more popular" approach of Franciscan preaching versus the "more formal" of the Dominican.[15] Furthermore, during periods of plague, famine, and conflict, Mary's representation became more attuned to the local people's needs and tended to be "more 'mother' than 'queen,' interceding with her son on behalf of her friends."[16]

Emerging in Local Colors

The dispersal of Marian devotion beyond Europe into mission territories prepared the stage for greater localization of Marian practices. In many instances, Marian practices simply took on minor adaptations such as literal translation into the local languages but closely retained its original form from Europe. In other cases, however, the impulse toward localization brought about more profound transformations, due to either missionary intentions or social dynamics in new contexts. Examples of these profound localizations are found first during the missionary movement from the sixteenth century onward and then in the so-called Age of Mary starting in the nineteenth century.

Through colonization, Catholic missionaries brought Mary's figure into the uncharted social landscapes of American highlands and Asian coastal settlements. For example, between the sixteenth and nineteenth centuries in the colonial Philippines, Spanish religious orders brought their Marian devotions to their assigned mission stations and parishes. Thus "Mary presided over communities in various incarnations and iconographies, terrestrially rooted, each possessing its own discrete titles, powers, and legends."[17] Though intended to be nothing more than part of the traditional missionary enterprise of "transplanting of the church" from European Christendom, many practices incorporated local cultural resources. In colonial Philippines, the generic Dominican *Nuestra Señora del Santísimo Rosario* (Our Lady of the Most Holy Rosary) became known in terms of its specific parish locations such as Piat (Cagayan) or Manaoag (Pangasinan). Moreover, "many of these titles were in the local languages, taking on place names (Our Lady of Namacpacan), connoting common forms of livelihood (Our Lady of Salambao, where *salambao* is a fisherman's net), or flora and fauna (Our Lady of Caysasay, named after a species of bird known as *casay-casay*)."[18]

Apart from this translation into local languages, which was in line with the decision of the Synod of Manila in 1582 to evangelize the Philippines using its local languages, the localization of these Marian devotions was more than superficial.[19] Local cultural ethos as well as everyday situations shaped the form of these practices. Traditional Marian iconography was modified; stories of unexpected discoveries of Marian statues by the seashore or atop tall trees became part of local religious lore. De la Cruz writes, "The diversity of devotional practices that flourished around each of these icons and the miracles attributed to them demonstrated that sacredness was plural and deeply tethered to, if not immanent in, the material representation (the image, or *santo*, in vernacularized Spanish), which in turn was attached to the land and geographically bound."[20]

The most enduring but also the most complex exemplar of these localized Marian devotions would be the cult to Our Lady of Guadalupe, which began in 1581 with apparitions in Tepeyac, Mexico, to a poor indigenous baptized Juan Diego and is still popular today within the church and beyond. From the beginning, it has been woven from multiple strands from both indigenous and Christian resources, historical documentation and oral tradition, colonial and nationalist sentiments, church and state authorities, and others—hence, its inherently complex and continuously contested nature.

D. A. Brading appropriately entitled his comprehensive study *Mexican Phoenix*: [on the one hand], "for the Church at large, Our Lady of Guadalupe is simply a Mexican representation of the Virgin Mary, Mother of God, and…in her sanctuary the faithful attend the same Eucharistic service, hear the same scriptural readings and receive the same communion as can be found in any other Catholic Church throughout the world. On the other hand, the changes in the way the Virgin has been presented and interpreted reflect the equally profound changes in Mexican society across the centuries."[21] Both these faces are mirrored in the most central features of its iconography and devotion; for instance, the name Guadalupe's supposed origins from Spanish or Nahuatl,[22] and the visual references to the native goddess Tonantzin and other traditional Marian titles.[23] What remains at the core of this devotion, however, is the unmistakable localized countenance of Mary's figure as *indígena* (native) as far as her skin tone and facial features are concerned.

Beyond the indigenization of Mary's figure, this impulse toward localization has been expressed in other ways, particularly from the period known as "the Age of Mary" from the nineteenth century onward.[24] Historical studies associate this development with the emerging Marian devotions in France; Mary's figure appeared in 1830 to the nun Catherine Labouré at the Sisters of Charity chapel in Paris; in 1846, to children Mélanie Calvat and Maximin Giraud at the Alpine hamlet La Salette-Fallavaux; and in 1858 to fourteen-year-old Bernadette Soubirous at a Lourdes cave-grotto below the Pyrenees. These and other subsequent Marian devotions attracted much attention because of their profound links to their corresponding historical contexts.

Though such links existed in earlier devotions such as Our Lady of Guadalupe and appear pronounced in relatively more recent instances, probably because of more available historical documentation, the extensive and deeper links to historical context must not be underestimated. Not only are these devotions immersed in the social dynamics of their contemporary church and world, but they explicitly or implicitly addressed these contexts.

This profound link to historical context is manifested through "messages" to and involvement in their social milieu. First, though messages from the devotions differ in content and form, they address existing situations, either through words to witnesses or in symbolic expressions. For instance, in contrast to self-referential concerns about building shrines in many late medieval apparitions, Mary's first message to Catherine Labouré spoke of the contemporary state of France just a few days before the July Revolution: that "the throne will be overturned"; that "among the clergy of Paris there will be victims"; and that "the cross will be despised, it will be trampled under foot… the streets will flow with blood."[25] Beyond the prophetic foreboding, its significance lies in "the nature of the communications, in that Mary makes explicit reference to events that shall take place in what we would consider modern historical time. She does not only appear *in* the world but also speaks *about* the world."[26]

Perhaps best known among such messages would be the three-part "secret" of Our Lady of Fatima given to shepherd children, Lúcia dos Santos and her cousins Jacinta and Francisco Marto, during the First World War and the virulent influenza pandemic in 1918–19. In 1944, church authorities made public the first two parts from then Carmelite nun Lúcia's accounts, which refer to hell's torments, devotion to the Immaculate Heart of Mary, World War II, and the rise of Russian Communism. Only on April 19, 2000, would Pope John Paul II unseal the third part with accompanying documentation from the Congregation of the Doctrine of the Faith (CDF).[27] Though much awaited within Catholic circles, this part rehearses earlier themes about the dire need for repentance, evils of Russian Communism, and great sufferings for all the church, including the pope; this last was understood as referring to the May 13, 1981, assassination attempt on Pope John Paul II.

These messages from Marian devotions, whether explicit or not and in reference to specific events in the future or social situations in general, speak with alarming concern for a suffering church and a world in crisis; hence the universal call to repentance and conversion in many Marian devotions even without claims of apparitions or auditions. This global concern is thus reflected in the CDF statement on Fatima: "The twentieth century was one of the most crucial in human history, with its tragic and cruel events culminating in the assassination attempt on 'the sweet Christ on earth.' Now a veil is drawn back on a series of events which make history and interpret it in depth, in a spiritual perspective alien to present-day attitudes, often tainted with rationalism."[28]

This important manifestation of the link of Marian devotions to historical context indicates how deeply immersed they are in the social dynamics of their settings even in the absence of messages about them. For instance, in Mart Bax's study of the origins of the phenomenon of Medjugorje through the apparitions of 1981, its global popularity as a pilgrimage site, and its subsequent diminishment, this profound historical link is evident in relation to long-standing conflicts: the enduring struggle between the Franciscan religious order and diocesan bishops over parishes, the violent "little war" between feuding local families and clans, and the historic "great war" between ethnic Serbs and Croatians.[29] Thus, the Medjugorje phenomenon could not be understood apart from these violent and conflict-ridden social dynamics. With the resumption of the pilgrimage in 1992, "when the gunpowder had settled…it was only in the eyes of the pilgrims that everything seemed the same as before"; but "the people of Medjugorje knew, a hatred smouldered that would one day be sparked into flame again."[30]

William Christian's *Visionaries: The Spanish Republic and the Reign of Christ* provides an even more comprehensive account of profound links to social dynamics in his analysis of the visions in 1931 at Ezkioga in the tumultuous Basque region just before the Spanish Civil War: "As a mass phenomenon, the apparitions at Ezkioga were a kind of dialogue between divinities and the anti-clerical left—anarchists and socialists in the Basque coastal cities, socialist farmworkers in Navarra, republican railway officials, and schoolteachers in rural areas, anti-clerical poor in cities throughout Spain, and socialist and communist movements worldwide."[31] Thus, the study focuses not only on one but "two kinds of visionaries and their interrelationships: the seers (*videntes*, in Spanish; *ikusleak*, in Basque) who had visions of Mary and the saints and the believers and promoters who had a vision of the future which they hope Mary and the saints would confirm."[32]

Christian charts the tortuous path of this complex phenomenon throughout the twentieth century, following its many characters from traditional Catholicism, partisan journalism, ecclesiastical offices, and competing ideologies. Even before the multiple visions began, the content of their messages was already suggested in the press, for example, in the *El Día* of July 31: "Let the Mother of Heaven make her decisions manifest, for we her sons in Gipuzkoa are prepared to carry them out."[33]

But despite how deeply the Ezkioga devotion was embroiled in conflict-driven social dynamics, Christian rejects any reductive assessment, whether in terms of partisan political manipulation, ecclesiastical defense against modernity, or personal psychological needs.[34] He subverts explanatory binary oppositions of rural versus urban, or female and children versus male clerics, which, though present in the Ezkioga events, were inadequate accounts.[35] Instead, he connects them with "visions of the divine [that] are as old as humanity….The visions at Ezkioga in 1931 reflect a phase in the history of Western society and in the place of Catholic divinities in that society."[36] They form "part of a skein of divine intervention" that weaves through time and space, and threads fundamental questions about life and death, made urgent and burning during critical times as at Ezkioga.[37] Individuals and groups, usually with mixed allegiances, sought answers to deeply felt questions; for individuals, "What will happen to me when I die? Why did disaster strike me? What will occur tomorrow?"[38] and for groups, "Was the Virgin appearing to a virtuous Basque Country or a sinful Spain?

Were there sins enough in the Basque Country, with its working-class indifference and sybaritic beaches, to provoke her tears?"[39]

Though Christian remains reticent on whether Catholicism in general and the Ezkioga phenomenon in particular have provided compelling answers, he nevertheless considers his work "as a memorial to their spiritual adventure."[40] His significant contribution lies in recognizing that Ezkioga and other similar phenomena before and after show the enduring reality of how "people interact with the gods and with one another."[41]

Christian's study does not lead to a theological dead-end; it provides an opening to further theological exploration of Marian devotion. The related dynamic between its transhistorical and localizing impulses points to the perennial interwoven thread of divine-human interaction within changing historical seasons and geographies, especially during crises for society and the church, and times of great need such as pestilence and natural calamities. This pathway explores the theological significance of this dynamic within the unfolding of Christian tradition as played out in varying historical contexts.

Treading a Theological Path

Being an integral part of Christian tradition as well as traditioning, Marian devotions and many other instances of lived Christianity have been theologically accounted for under the rubric of inculturation and other similar vocabularies such as indigenization or contextualization. As noted in chapter 5, such considerations are useful if these are not regarded as monolithic and unidirectional, that is, not as the *translatio* of a ready-made gospel into a specific context. These processes are multidirectional and multifaceted encounters between historically mediated forms of Christianity, such as those brought by evangelizing missions, and the particular social ethos and dynamics of new contexts.

Given this, the path toward the theological significance of these practices of lived Christianity involves relating the mariological to the pneumatological as well as the local to the iconic or, in technical language, sublating the first term into the wider second.

First, the sublation of the mariological into the pneumatological overcomes the usual temptation of any Mariology to focus on Mary's figure in isolation and, second, it enriches the appropriate Vatican II stress on Mariology's relation to Christology. In either case, Mary's status as "being overshadowed by the Spirit" is duly recognized.

The dynamic between the transhistorical and localizing impulses in Marian devotion indicates that Mary's figure is more than the biblical Mary. This claim moves beyond conclusions of historical-critical study and into the unfolding of Mary's figure in new times and locations. As Orlando Espín asks in the context of Latino Catholicism: "Don't we face a need to rethink the contents of these devotions in(to) pneumatological categories (*"vertir" las devociones y categorías supestamente marianas, y sus contenidos, en categorías pneumatólogicas*), instead of continuing to insist on the Mary of Nazareth connection, in spite of this connection's historical absence among everyday people?" or "Why can't we understand the 'Mary' categories of Latino Catholicism as *orthodox popular pneumatology*?"[42] In raising these questions, he implies neither that "Mary of Nazareth (and, consequently Marian devotion) might just be mediating the maternal or feminine face of God, as some theologians have suggested" nor that "Mary *is* the Holy Spirit."[43]

On the contrary, such questions address the revelatory character of Marian devotions as part of Christian tradition under the Spirit's guidance. These devotions are traditionally considered private revelation different from public revelation in both degree and essence as far as the singularity, completeness, and normativity of God's revelation in Jesus Christ are concerned. According to the recent CDF document on Fatima,

> The term "public Revelation" refers to the revealing action of God directed to humanity as a whole and which finds its literary expression in the two parts of the Bible: The Old and New Testaments. It is called "Revelation" because in it God gradually made himself known to men, to the point of becoming man himself, in order to draw to himself the whole world and unite it with himself through his Incarnate Son, Jesus Christ.[44]

Private revelations differ in that "it is not their role to complete Christ's definitive Revelation, but to help live more fully by it in a certain period of history" (*CCC* §67).[45] Moreover, the commentary links them to the

Vatican II emphasis on "the signs of the times": "To interpret the signs of the times in the light of faith means to recognize the presence of Christ in every age. In the private revelations approved by the Church—and therefore also in Fatima—this is the point: they help us to understand the signs of the times and to respond to them rightly in faith."[46]

Essential though these differences between public and private revelations are, they do not negate the same fundamental dynamic structure of revelation in both. As suggested in chapter 5, God's historical self-disclosure to humankind is expressed through and received in the material, symbolic, and conceptual resources of the social context within which such revelation occurs. Thus, Christian Scripture presents the history of salvation through these resources, narrating God revealing through the prophets and in Jesus Christ, as well as Israel and the apostolic church receiving and transmitting this revelation in faith.

Given this historically mediated character of revelation, private revelation such as Marian devotions, even if not public revelation, is characterized by the same dynamic structure. Being part of the work of the Spirit in tradition, these devotions point to both how and what God reveals through them as well as how the faithful receive and transmit them—both employing the communicative resources in their historical contexts and, according to Vatican II, helping the faithful understand the signs of the times and live more fully revelation in Christ in a certain period of history.

Thus, Espín draws out the theological significance of Juan Diego's description of Mary's figure that draws from both Nahua Tonantzin, the cruel native goddess, and Christian Marian iconography: "Juan Diego's Mary assumes the symbols that are useful for Christianity but rejects those that could identify her with the old religion or that appear to at least condone it" and "precisely *because* Juan Diego claimed to have seen Mary *the way* he did, we can say today that this is a sign that the Christian gospel was in fact announced and accepted in early colonial Mexico."[47] Such an observation about the missionary evangelization of Mexico also applies to other similar contexts such as the Philippines, in which Christianity, though riding the sixteenth-century tides of colonialism and often tainted by this association, was profoundly translated into a social language that empowered the native population to worship the Christian God in and with their own tongues.[48]

In further elaborating how this historically mediated missionary preaching communicated God's revelation and was received in faith,

Espín borrows the concept of analogy often used in medieval Scholasticism and intended as "a way of speaking the unsayable Mystery."[49] Moreover, "all analogies—including effective analogies are always contextualized in history and culture, 'said' intelligibly within their various internal conflicts and power asymmetries (which consequently and inescapably, limit the intelligibility of each analogy to the specific contexts within which it is employed) and are never literal or symmetric with regards to the Mystery."[50]

This semantic and cultural—rather than ontological—analogy opens the possibility of linking Marian devotions to God's revelation. Thus, Espín's rhetorical questions: "Can analogy (semantic and cultural, *not* ontological) legitimately help us speak (in the manner of the semantic, cultural analogy) of God and the Christ? Could Mary be considered, in that sense, an analogy of *some* dimensions or attributes that Christians have discovered—as a gift of the Spirit—in the one they call God?"[51]

In other words, the work of the Spirit in God's self-disclosure and its reception are faithfully expressed through the communicative languages of new contexts—the same dynamic present, not only throughout Christian missionary evangelization but also in "the development of Christian perception and progressive acceptance of the revelation of God."[52]

This does not imply that the Guadalupe and other Marian devotions add something to the revelation in Christ. Often their "iconography has adequately communicated revelation, with contents authentically coherent with the text of the Bible and with other written documents of the Tradition."[53] Thus to the final rhetorical question: "Could the Virgin of Guadalupe be understood as a step—albeit an extremely important one—in the inculturation of the Tradition in Mexican (and later Mexican-American) history?"[54] Espín responds, "Catholic pneumatology and ecclesiology should have little difficulty today in affirming this role for Mary."[55]

Mary's figure as Our Lady of Guadalupe could then be characterized as mediating the encounter between Christian tradition as brought through missionary evangelization and the religious world of the indigenous Mexican people. With her, the multidirectional and multifaceted process of inculturation has commenced, and Christian revelation is communicated and received in faith. Given this, Our Lady of Guadalupe is not just mariological but truly pneumatological.

From the Local to the Iconic

Through the work of the Spirit in the devotion to Our Lady of Guadalupe, Christian revelation has been mediated not only to Juan Diego and those initial believers in his vision; this originary local experience has been received by succeeding generations of Christians in Hispanic America and beyond. This is reflected in the increasing recognition of her patronage through the centuries: patron of Mexico through the bull of Pope Benedict XIV issued on May 25, 1754; of all Latin America at a liturgical celebration in Rome on December 12, 1933; and of North and South America during the visit to Tepeyac, in March 1999, of Pope John Paul II, who later canonized Juan Diego on July 31, 2002.[56]

In this subsequent transmission of Christian tradition, the reception of the Guadalupe devotion has shifted from being local Christian practice into what Ricoeur refers to as the iconic. He draws its meaning not from the Eastern Christian tradition but from the seventeenth-century masters of the Dutch Golden Age who were "able to write a new text of reality" that is "neither the reproduction nor the production of the universe, but its metamorphosis."[57] In this sense, iconocity "means the revelation of a real more real than ordinary reality."[58]

Given Ricoeur's understanding of social practice as text, the originary Guadalupe devotion could be understood as iconic text, which, when transmitted to and received in new periods and geographies, prove revelatory by revealing meanings in these contexts. Going further toward "a theological interpretation of the image and its devotion,"[59] Brading references Catholic magisterial documents and, more significantly, the tradition of icons in the Orthodox Church, expressed by Basil the Great: "What the word transmits through the eye, that painting shows through the image…by these two means accompanying one another…we receive knowledge of the one and the same thing."[60]

Given this equivalence of word and image, Brading states, "In the same way that, through the Holy Spirit, Mary conceived and brought forth Christ into the world, so also, by the power of the Spirit, the Church strives through its members to incarnate Christ across the centuries and among all nations" and the Guadalupe image of Mary becomes recognized as "among the most potent expressions of the Holy Spirit in the long history of the Catholic Church."[61]

It is not surprising, therefore, that Our Lady of Guadalupe has not remained a local devotion but has become iconic: "From the time that the Guadalupe was first seen until the present day, the image has evoked the devotion and strengthened the faith of countless Mexicans. Instinctively saluted as 'Our Mother of Guadalupe' and even, in Mexican style, as 'the little mother,' the Virgin of Tepeyac acts like a magnet, as Siguenza y Góngora affirmed, silently generating a power which attracts millions of pilgrims to a sanctuary where the Eucharist is daily offered for their benefit."[62]

During his 1990 visit to Tepeyac, Pope John Paul II extended the iconic function of the Guadalupe image to Juan Diego at his beatification: "In the likeness of the ancient biblical personages, who were collective representations of all the people, we can say that Juan Diego represents all the natives who welcomed the Gospel of Jesus, thanks to the maternal assistance of Mary."[63]

This extension of the Guadalupe devotion into other contexts on account of its iconic character could be recognized as manifesting the work of the Spirit in the transmission of tradition. Because Our Lady of Guadalupe and other images "attract pilgrims; figure as patrons of cities, provinces and nations; exert a power over the faithful,"[64] Brading even dares to compare them to the inspired text of Scripture.

This iconic function of giving rise to meaning in new contexts is echoed in Gadamer's analysis of the classical text. In contrast to its usual characterization as artistic excellence deemed normative for others, "the classical is what is preserved precisely because it signifies and interprets itself; i.e., that which speaks in such a way that it is not a statement about what is past, a mere testimony to something that still needs to be interpreted but says something to the present as if it were said specially to it. What we call 'classical' does not first require the overcoming of historical distance, for in its own constant communication it does overcome it. The classical, then, is certainly 'timeless,' but this timelessness is a mode of historical being."[65]

When seen in terms of the iconic, even the classical in Gadamer's sense, the Guadalupe and other devotions are appropriately considered to "say something to a new context as if specifically said to it." Hence, these religious practices, though originating from a particular situation, could continue to be vibrant and relevant in and to other contexts. What they express is generated in their encounter with these contexts, which are distinct in their differences and shaped by their religious concerns, particular social dynamics, and other characteristics. Thus, the work of the Spirit unfolds in interaction with these defining characteristics, including the often contentious social dynamics, in Fatima, Ezkioga, and Medjugorje.

The iconic character of Marian devotions in new contexts could uncover nuances in the meaning of these devotions. Elements previously implicit or newly discovered appear in greater focus. For instance, Carmen Nanko-Fernandez notes how "other Hispanic theologians have described Mary's figure in many ways, but they nevertheless recognize her as a symbolic expression of God's self-disclosure."[66] She cites Miguel Diaz for support: "Whether understood as the female face of God (Rodriguez, Elizondo), a symbol of the Holy Spirit (Espín), the poetry of the Trinitarian God (Garcia), or the *mestizo* face of the divine (Goizueta), it is clear that US Hispanic theologians understand Marian symbols as mediators of the life of grace, especially to and within the experience of the poor and marginalized."[67]

Furthermore, as is evident in the development of Christian tradition, "what might be *clearly* true and/or accepted at a given age or a given place in Church history might not have been so at an earlier period *or at a different place* in the same history, sometimes provoking (or having been provoked by) confrontation about a (better) understanding of truth or about the way the latter is being expressed."[68] For instance, the title "Mediatrix of All Grace" has been occasionally present in Marian devotion and literature but has remained obscure. However, its recent association with the apparitions in 1948 at a Carmelite monastery in the Philippine town of Lipa, Batangas, and its active promotion as the fifth Marian dogma have generated controversy because it could undermine Christ's role as the sole mediator between God and humankind.[69] On account of this and other factors surrounding the apparitions, the CDF did not give official recognition despite earlier approval from the local hierarchy.

One finds another instance of nuances emerging in new contexts in the Our Lady of the Pillar devotion in the southern Philippine city of Zamboanga, long subject to tensions between indigenous, Christian, and Muslim inhabitants. Though inspired by the early Spanish devotion at Zaragoza based on Mary's alleged appearance to the apostle James, the bas-relief of Mary apparently clad in native dress was installed in 1734 above the eastern gate of a fort reconstructed to ward off Muslim slave raids.[70] Since then, the shrine has been linked to miracle stories and is visited by both Christians and Muslims alike, seeking cures for the sick and protection from calamities. According to recent fieldwork, some Muslim pilgrims, though aware of its Catholic origins and hence *haram* (forbidden) in Islamic tradition, allege that Mary first appeared to Muslims but, upon being rejected, proceeded to Christians.[71] Having Muslims and Christians praying side by side has been recognized as a possible venue for dialogue.

These examples illustrating how varying nuances of Marian practices emerge in new contexts indicate the iconic function based on the pneumatological character of Marian devotion. Propelled by trans-historical and localizing impulses in the reception and transmission of Christian tradition, they reflect the work of the Holy Spirit in communicating God's self-disclosure to the faithful in and through the human and historical character of these contexts.

Such incarnate sublation of grace and nature is not exclusive to Marian devotion but is also reflected in other devotional practices of Christian tradition. According to Espín, "These expressions [e.g., Crucified Christ] are not part of the normative Tradition of the Church. But the faith intuitions behind them most certainly, are…the passion symbols of Latino popular Catholicism not only do not hinder the building up of the Reign but, in fact, preach solidarity and compassion as attitudes of the Crucified God that are also expected from Christians."[72]

Thus, seen with "the eyes of faith" and marked by their pneumatological and iconic character, the status of these religious practices embedded in contexts characterized by multiple and often conflicting forces does not occasion disedification but calls for faithful attentiveness. This will be discussed in the next chapter.

7

Lived Christianity as *Sensus Fidei*

GIVEN ITS DYNAMIC and inclusive quality, Christian tradition encompasses "*everything* that contributes to making the people of God live their lives in holiness and grow in faith," and this includes particular devotional traditions (*Dei Verbum* 8). Through its illustrative discussion of different traditional examples of Marian devotion, the preceding chapter has demonstrated the vibrant nature of lived Christianity, in particular, of how religious practices embody Christians' faith in their everyday life and context. But not all forms of Marian devotion in the previous chapter share the same significance and reception within Christian tradition and in relation to Christian faith.

Though devotional practice is part of Christian tradition as expressing the faith of those engaged in them as well as the wider Christian community, greater attentiveness and discernment is called for regarding the status and recognition of each particular practice. In Ormond Rush's reckoning, this process falls under the general rubric of spiritual reception, that is, "both the personal appropriation of revelation and the assent to the content of 'the faith' by believers, as they [the baptized] attempt to adhere to, penetrate and apply it to their daily lives (*LG* 12)."[1]

This process of attentiveness and discernment could be implicit or explicit and informal or official, depending on circumstances. Some traditions experience transformation into quasi-ideology or disappear with dwindling support. Others are criticized and even condemned as inadequate for or distorting of Christian faith in terms of their theological views, ethical norms, and practical implications. In all these instances, the value and significance of religious practices as well as the corresponding degree of reception remain subject to various forms of discernment by the people of God and its members.

This chapter focuses on this ecclesial process of discernment regarding certain religious practices. It employs the understanding of the *sensus fidei* as a cornerstone in analyzing this process of discernment and the 2014 International Theological Commission (ITC) document, *Sensus Fidei in the Life of the Church*.[2] Like many official church texts initiated by and produced through corporate discussion, this document's intent is limited; it aims "not to give an exhaustive account of the *sensus fidei*, but simply to clarify and deepen some important aspects of this vital notion in order to respond to certain issues, particularly regarding how to identify the authentic *sensus fidei* in situations of controversy" (no. 6). It focuses, therefore, on "approbative reception": "the process of evaluation by the whole church in judging whether particular spiritual, juridical, or theological receptions are faithful to revelation."[3]

While cognizant of "juridical reception"—the official institutional processes involved in recognizing a particular religious practice as part of the faith of the church—this chapter instead provides a wider pastoral-theological account of this ecclesial process and how Christians live their faith in their everyday life and contexts.

This perspective on sensing the faith of the people of God puts lived Christianity at its center and, as McGuire notes, highlights its "embodied practices" that are embedded in people's social and interior lives and are characterized by practical rather than theoretical rationality (see chapter 2).[4] Moreover, it engages the lively conversation between ecclesiology and ethnography "in the struggle to find ways of speaking *both* of the church as described in the Christian tradition *and* of the real, lived experience of Christian communal life and work" and thus "to speak truthfully about concrete realities and faithfully about the historical and present promise of the work of the Spirit, enlivening what we understand to be 'the body of Christ,' the church."[5] This conversation contextualizes the *sensus fidei* in Christian tradition, provides a sketch of the church as imperfect and pilgrim, and promotes the strategic approach of sensing the faith "from below" and "at the peripheries."

Seeing with the Eyes of Faith

Though the term *sensus fidei* is of recent vintage, the first chapter of the ITC document takes great pains and many paragraphs to show that its meaning has been operative in the texts of both Scripture and tradition (*Sensus Fidei* 7–47). Its basic nomenclature makes the following important distinctions: first, between "the sense *for* the faith," referring to an active orientation, and "the sense *of* the faith," meaning what that faith consists in; and second, between individual believers and the whole church as historical subjects of the *sensus fidei*.

Given these distinctions, the document provides insights relevant to the process of approbative reception of religious practices. First, it links the *sensus fidei* as active orientation and other analogous expressions such as "supernatural instinct" (e.g., *Sensus Fidei* 2), "second nature" (e.g., no. 53), and "connaturality" (e.g., no. 50) to the historical unfolding of God's revelation and of its transmission in tradition.

Drawing from the Second Vatican Council's *Lumen Gentium* and *Dei Verbum*, it states that "the *sensus fidei* is presented as Christ's gift to the faithful, and once again is described as an active capacity by which the faithful are able to understand, live, and proclaim the truths of divine revelation. It is the basis for their work of evangelization" (*Sensus Fidei* 45). Moreover, this active capacity "is also evoked in the council's teaching on the development of doctrine, in the context of the transmission of the apostolic faith. *Dei Verbum* says that the apostolic Tradition 'makes progress in the Church, with the help of the Holy Spirit'" (*Sensus Fidei* 46).

In relation to this, Rush borrows the image of "the eyes of faith" from Augustine, Aquinas, and other theologians (*Sensus Fidei* 45) and identifies it as "the organon of the *sensus fidei*" (no. 45). Thus the *sensus fidei* refers not only to the sense of sight of the church and its members but also to what they see with the eyes of faith, "enabling the one church throughout the world to receive revelation faithfully and meaningfully, and then to tradition it effectively."[6]

Through the eyes of faith functioning as organon of the *sensus fidei*, approbative discernment of religious practices occurs concurrently and produces "the resulting sense or meaning or interpretation which individual Christians or the community as a whole make of the faith, consciously or unconsciously, explicitly, or implicitly."[7] Thus, recognition or rejection of a particular practice could be explicit and reflexive through specific processes, or implicit and unthematized through continued use. Moreover, throughout this process, which involves church members, "patience and respect are needed in their mutual interactions if the *sensus fidei* is to be clarified and a true *consensus fidelium*, a *conspiratio pastorum et fidelium*, is to be achieved" (*Sensus Fidei* 71).

Moreover, these "eyes of faith" belong to the historical subjects of Christian tradition, to all believers—lay as well as those with technical or official roles. This character, the ITC document insists, traces back to the Second Vatican Council: "Banishing the caricature of an active hierarchy and a passive laity, and in particular the notion of a strict separation between the teaching Church (*ecclesia docens*) and the learning Church (*ecclesia discens*), the council taught that all the baptized participate in their own proper way in the three offices of Christ as prophet, priest and king" (*Sensus Fidei* 4).[8] In particular, *Lumen Gentium* "teaches that, 'until the full manifestation of his glory,' the Lord fulfills this office 'not only by the hierarchy who teach in his name and by his power, but also by the laity.' With regard to the latter, it continues: 'He accordingly both establishes them as witnesses and provides them with the appreciation of the faith and the grace of the word [*sensus fidei et gratia verbi instruit*] (cf. Acts 2:17–18; Apoc 19:10) so that the power of the Gospel may shine out in daily family and social life'" (*Sensus Fidei* 45). As "Christ's gift to the faithful," the *sensus fidei* is "an active capacity by which the faithful are able to understand, live and proclaim the truths of divine revelation" (no. 45).

All the baptized, therefore, participate in the approbative task of the *sensus fidei*. It is in this context that the ITC document surprisingly speaks of the infallibility of the *sensus fidei* without undermining that of the magisterial office. In its survey of related theological views, it cites Congar: "'The Church loving and believing, that is, the body of the faithful, is infallible in the living possession of the faith, not in a particular act or judgment'" (no. 43). Moreover, it affirms "the idea that the Church as a whole is infallible in her belief, since she is the body and bride of Christ (cf. 1 Cor 12:27; Eph 4:12; 5:21–32; Rev 21:9), and that all of her members have an anointing that teaches them (cf. 1 John 2:20, 27), being endowed with the Spirit of truth (cf. John 16:13), is everywhere apparent from the very beginnings of Christianity" (no. 7). Though distinct from official magisterial infallibility, "the *sensus fidei fidelis* [the sense of faith of the faithful] is infallible in itself with regard to its object: the true faith," thus indicating the theological significance of lived Christianity (no. 55).

Searching Together for the Faith

In contrast to the earlier 2012 ITC document, "Theology Today: Perspectives, Principles and Criteria," which was drafted by the same authors as the 2014 document, the latter document on the *sensus fidei* is, according to Gerard Mannion, "more direct and less ambivalent" in emphasizing the Second Vatican Council's teaching on the importance of the *sensus fidei* in the life of the Church.[9] As noted in chapter 5 regarding Christian tradition, the whole Church is both a passive and an active historical subject in relation to apostolic and ecclesial traditions respectively.

Thus, the dynamic and perennial process of sensing the faith calls for a church that is both learning and teaching. The ITC document then appropriately criticizes the "strict separation between the teaching Church (*ecclesia docens*) and the learning Church (*ecclesia discens*)," especially when correlated with the distinction between the hierarchical magisterium and the lay faithful (see *Sensus Fidei* 4).

In searching together for the sense of the faith, both listening and teaching are inherent tasks of all the baptized, encompassing three sectors—the majority laity, those with theological expertise, and the magisterium. Though members of each sector are engaged on account of their common fundamental bond as baptized, each sector has specific roles in the process of approbative discernment.

First, the role of the lay faithful comes from their knowledge from living the faith: "It is a knowledge by empathy, or a knowledge of the heart" (*Sensus Fidei* 50). Derived from "the concrete reality of the existential situations in which he or she is placed by family, professional and cultural relations," this knowledge "enriches the personal experience of the believer" and "enables him or her to see more precisely the value and the limits of a given doctrine, and to propose ways of refining its formulation" (no. 54). Its specific tasks are described as follows: "1) to discern whether or not a particular teaching or practice that they actually encounter in the Church is coherent with the true faith by which they live in the communion of the Church; 2) to distinguish in what is preached between the essential and the secondary; and 3) to determine and put into practice the witness to Jesus Christ that they should give in the particular historical and cultural context in which they live" (no. 60).

At the same time, certain dispositions are deemed necessary for authentic lay engagement in the *sensus fidei*: participation in the life of the church, listening to the Word of God, openness to reason, adherence to the magisterium, holiness shown through humility, freedom, and joy, and seeking the edification of the church (see nos. 88–105). Though these dispositions are certainly important, they are best seen as desired ideals rather than rigid requirements. As in our discussion on Christian identity in chapter 5, there are those among the baptized who may not meet all these dispositions without moral culpability.

According to Rush, "Catholics who are inactive, lapsed, disaffected, or marginalized in the church" could be "the secondary source for determining the faith of the church," and "to ignore the perspective of this group is to miss the opportunity for ecclesial learning not only with regard to how to reach out more effectively to such individuals, but also with regard to prophetic intuitions which may well indicate inchoate development of doctrine."[10] Moreover, this more inclusive spirit in sensing the faith of the church is even suggested in the ITC document's recognition of the possible contribution of other Christians (see *Sensus Fidei* 86), whom Rush refers to as "an ancillary source."[11]

Second, the role of the theological community—composed of ordained seminary teachers before Vatican II but of more lay men and women after—derives from their expertise. Distinct from the laity's knowledge of the heart, the theological community engaged in *scientia fidei* offers "reflective knowledge of the mysteries of faith which deploys concepts and uses rational procedures to reach its conclusions" (*Sensus Fidei* 54). Due to their expertise rather than to clerical office, they share in the teaching task of the church but are equally obliged to "depend and reflect on the *sensus fidelium*" (nos. 81–84).

On the one hand, "theology steeps itself in the reality of the apostolic Tradition which underlies and overflows the strict bounds of the statements in which the teaching of the Church is formulated, because it comprises 'all that she herself is, all that she believes'" (no. 83). On the other hand, "theology needs to provide principles and criteria for its discernment, particularly by the magisterium. Through critical inquiry, theologians help to reveal and to clarify the content of the *sensus fidelium*, 'recognising and demonstrating that issues relating to the truth of faith can be complex, and that investigation of them must be precise'" (no. 83).

Third, as these examples indicate, the magisterium as a corporate teaching office plays an integral twofold role in searching for the faith of the church. Though "the baptised cannot be passive" and "have received the Spirit and are endowed as members of the body of the Lord with gifts and charisms 'for the renewal and building up of the Church,' so the magisterium has to be attentive to the *sensus fidelium*, the living voice of the people of God. Not only do they have the right to be heard, but their reaction to what is proposed as belonging to the faith of the Apostles must be taken very seriously, because it is by the Church as a whole that the apostolic faith is borne in the power of the Spirit" (no. 74). Thus, "the magisterium does not have sole responsibility for it" (no. 74).

At the same time, however, "the magisterium nurtures, discerns, and judges the *sensus fidelium* as "those 'who have received, along with their right of succession in the episcopate, the sure charism of truth'" (no. 76). Moreover, it "also judges with authority whether opinions which are present among the people of God, and which may seem to be the *sensus fidelium*, actually correspond to the truth of the Tradition received from the Apostles" (no. 77). The exercise of such authority, far from absolute, takes different forms and degrees of normativity.[12]

The ITC document illustrates this searching together by the lay faithful, the theological community, and the teaching office in relation to the dogmatic definition of Mary's Immaculate Conception. In relation to Pope Pius IX's apostolic constitution *Ineffabilis Deus* (1854) on the Immaculate Conception, it cites not only the influence of theologian Giovanni Perrone (1794–1876) but also the constitution's conclusion that "'Holy Scripture, venerable Tradition, the constant mind of the Church [*perpetuus Ecclesiae sensus*], the remarkable agreement of Catholic bishops and the faithful [*singularis catholicorum Antistitum ac fidelium conspiratio*], and the memorable Acts and Constitutions of our predecessors' all wonderfully illustrated and proclaimed the doctrine" (*Sensus Fidei* 38). This definition mentions the three distinct sectors within the church, but the attendant historical process has neither been straightforward nor clear-cut. Without diminishing the fundamental ground of this and other doctrinal matters, one recognizes that the lay faithful, the theological community, and those involved in the teaching office are not monolithic sectors and profess a plurality of views until such matters are declared an essential part of Christian faith.

As a result, Mannion, among others, has criticized the twofold function of the magisterium as "an ambiguity reminiscent of some of the tensions on key issues that were left unresolved also in the documents of Vatican II, particularly pertaining to questions of magisterium, collegiality, and the role of the faithful, among other issues."[13] Jeannine Fletcher even regards the Second Vatican Council's view of the *sensus fidelium* as "disingenuous insofar as the concept is not actually democratic, and dangerous in the promise of certainty that it holds."[14] Though both correctly trace the ITC document's "ambiguity" to Vatican II, one could ask whether this is an inherent character not only of church documents but also within Christianity itself. Though prominent in Catholicism because of its doctrine regarding the integral hierarchical nature of the church, the dynamic relationship between lay faithful, professional theologians, and those in the ministry of teaching, whether official or not, is unavoidably dialectical. Even the historical and recent experiences of churches belonging to the tradition of the Reformation and without an authoritative magisterium attest to this dialectical character.

Hence, much discussion on the *sensus fidei* and its underpinnings has taken place across different theological disciplines, including canon law.[15] Many provide nuanced readings of official documents and locate the *sensus fidei* at the core of Christian communion, so that the dialectical relations between laity, theological community, and magisterium are construed in the service of Christian life and mission.

Nevertheless, beneath these theological disagreements lie the common desire and call for an ethos of mutual recognition and communication that remains the sine qua non for searching together for the faith and requires ongoing conversion for the entire people of God. For example, the ITC document highlights the importance of respect among laity, theologians, and the magisterium based on "a genuine equality of dignity among all the faithful" and on their contribution, "each according to his or her own condition and office, to the building up of the Body of Christ" (*Sensus Fidei* 120).

Moreover, as invaluable members of the listening and teaching church, they all learn from and teach each other in sensing the faith of the church. Thus, in difficult times of disagreement and even resistance over particular teachings, the document further enjoins the faithful to "reflect on the teaching that has been given, making every effort to understand and accept it" and the magisterium as well to "reflect on the teaching that has been given and consider whether it needs clarification or reformulation in order to communicate more effectively the essential message," so that "these mutual efforts...express the communion that is essential to the life of the Church, and likewise a yearning for the grace of the Spirit who guides the Church 'into all the truth' (John 16:13)" (*Sensus Fidei* 80).

Differing situations, according to the ITC document, illustrate this dialectical interaction within the people of God: "Sometimes the people of God, and in particular the laity, intuitively felt in which direction the development of doctrine would go, even when theologians and bishops were divided on the issue. Sometimes there was a clear *conspiratio pastorum et fidelium*. Sometimes, when the Church came to a definition, the *Ecclesia docens* had clearly 'consulted' the faithful, and it pointed to the *consensus fidelium* as one of the arguments which legitimated the definition" (no. 72).

Processes and Structures for Consulting

Concurrent with continuing theological reflection toward greater precision and new insights on the dynamic interaction between church members and sectors, there is accompanying urgency to explore how sensing the faith operates in the communal experience and personal lives of Christians. Such an exploration into lived Christianity examines specific processes and structures underlying the discernment of the *sensus fidei*.

Though neither officially definitive nor theologically comprehensive, the ITC document itself points to some of these processes and structures in the contemporary ecclesial context. It notes the importance of and need for "consulting the faithful" (*Sensus Fidei* 121–26) and the value of "public exchange of opinion" as "a prime means by which, in a normal way, the *sensus fidelium* can be gauged" (no. 125). Thus "the Catholic Church is not afraid of discussion or controversy regarding her teaching. On the contrary, she welcomes debate as a manifestation of religious freedom. Everyone is free either to criticize or to support her. Indeed, she recognizes that fair and constructive critique can help her to see problems more clearly and to find better solutions" (no. 115). Such exchange is facilitated by greater participation and competence among the laity today as well as by wider communications networks within the church and beyond (see no. 115), enabling "many members of the Church [who] want to exercise their own competence, and to participate in their own proper way in the life of the Church" (no. 116).

Nevertheless, "there can be no simple identification between the *sensus fidei* and public or majority opinion" as "the *sensus fidei* is obviously related to faith, and faith is a gift not necessarily possessed by all people" (no. 118). The church recognizes democratic ideals in civil society, its inherent elements of disagreement, even dissent, and its resulting tension between majority and minority. But the church's self-understanding is never described in democratic terms, since "the Church, the mystery of the communion of humanity with God, receives her constitution from Christ. It is from him that she receives her internal structure and her principles of government" (no. 114).

Church consultation among members, therefore, is neither a democratic process nor majority public opinion. As the document insists, "the word 'consult' includes the idea of seeking a judgment or advice as well as inquiring into a matter of fact....When the magisterium is defining a doctrine, it is appropriate to consult the faithful in the sense of inquiring into a matter of fact, 'because the body of the faithful is one of the witnesses to the fact of the tradition of revealed doctrine, and because their consensus through Christendom is the voice of the Infallible Church'" (no. 121). The magisterium listens to as well as nurtures, discerns, and judges the *sensus fidelium* (see nos. 74–77) and "judges with authority whether opinions which are present among the people of God, and which may seem to be the *sensus fidelium*, actually correspond to the truth of the Tradition received from the Apostles" (no. 77).

Given this church process of consultation, the document enumerates structures of participation for sensing the faith:

> Various institutional instruments by which the faithful may more formally be heard and consulted have been established, such as particular councils, to which priests and others of Christ's faithful may be invited, diocesan synods, to which the diocesan bishop may also invite lay people as members, the pastoral council of each diocese, which is "composed of members of Christ's faithful who are in full communion

> with the Catholic Church: clerics, members of institutes of consecrated life, and especially lay people," and pastoral councils in parishes, in which "Christ's faithful, together with those who by virtue of their office are engaged in pastoral care in the parish, give their help in fostering pastoral action." (no. 125)

Furthermore, "they [the laity] organize themselves within parishes and in various groups and movements to build up the Church and to influence society at large, and they seek contact via social media with other believers and with people of good will" (no. 116). These structures of consultation "can be greatly beneficial to the Church, but only if pastors and lay people are mutually respectful of one another's charisms and if they carefully and continually listen to one another's experiences and concerns. Humble listening at all levels and proper consultation of those concerned are integral aspects of a living and lively Church" (no. 126).

Further exploration of how these ecclesial processes and structures operate on various levels of church life is called for and facilitated by contemporary research on the interface between theological ecclesiology and empirical ethnography, also referred to as "field work in theology" and "congregational studies."[16] Cognizant of earlier ethnographies of religious communities and of inherent tensions in multidisciplinarity,[17] those exploring this interface employ a more inclusive understanding of ethnography expressed by leading proponent Paul Fiddes as not just participant-observation of a closely defined group but also "other methods of investigation, such as short-term observation, interviews, analysis of speech patterns appearing in the discourse of the group, study of journals kept by members of the group, use of surveys (supplementing other means), and introduction into the group of texts to be read and reflected upon."[18] Put simply, Robert Orsi's question about a Chicago parish—"Where are the theologians from the seminaries on the South side, I want to know, with their talk of postmodernism and narrativity?"—fueled his desire "to attend to the experiences and beliefs of people in the midst of their lives, to encounter religion in its place in actual men and women's lived experience, in the place where they live and work."[19]

Such exploration on lived Christianity channels earlier views in practical or pastoral theology such as the "pastoral cycle" but also critiques their approaches as narrow deduction from or mere application of theological insights.[20]

Testing Processes and Structures of Participation

How these processes and structures operate in church communities and help in sensing the faith expressed in religious practice are illustrated in two well-known studies on post–Vatican II American Catholicism: Bradford Hinze on the Archdiocese of New York and Jerome Baggett on parishes in the San Francisco Bay Area.[21] Though not necessarily typical of ecclesial situations, they describe communal and personal experiences of parishioners, relate these descriptions of lived Christianity to theological accounts of the church, and thereby provide insights on how these processes and structures for consultation facilitate discernment toward approbative reception of religious practice.

Hinze's study—based on personal participation in parish life and on numerous interviews of laity, religious sisters, and pastors—focuses on the processes and structures referred to in the ITC document (parish and archdiocesan pastoral councils, senate of the clergy) as well as on other non–church-affiliated organizations such as the South Bronx People for Change and the Northwest Bronx Community and Clergy Coalition.[22]

At stake in the discernment underlying these processes and structures was the religious practice emerging in response to "Vatican II's invitation to become agents in history as a pilgrim people of God,"[23] which "motivated the implementation of structural innovations and reforms in the Archdiocese of New York, at the diocesan level, the parish level, the neighborhood level, and among priests and religious congregations."[24] Moreover, this emergent religious practice did not remain *ad intra* but also engaged wider social concerns: "People of the Bronx, Catholics, Protestants, Jews, and the religiously unaffiliated, led by coalitions of clergy, lay and secular leaders, and organizers, accomplished something remarkable. They joined together to confront powerful forces of destruction by building bonds of solidarity, by undertaking collective action for social justice, and by creating communal geographic and cultural oases of hope."[25]

By the mid-1980s however, the reception and development of this emergent religious practice faltered. The 1988 Archdiocesan Synod, which was systematically prepared for and based on extensive surveys, proved to be a turning point.[26] The three-day synod assembly of more than two hundred delegates discussed emerging concerns such as fostering lay leadership, increasing women's roles, and attending to ethnic and racial diversity. But those deemed controversial, even those "raised in the initial phone interviews, again on the written surveys, and during the synod itself...were not actively engaged during the synod; and any echo of them is filtered out of the final directives."[27]

Such change in reception, Hinze admits, is associated with but not reduced to two related developments during John Paul II's and Benedict XVI's pontificates: leadership changes in the New York Archdiocese and the Vatican as well as the promotion of communion ecclesiology by the Congregation for the Doctrine of the Faith.[28] Though the notion of communion is rooted in and integral to Vatican II's ecclesiological insights, this version sought to address perceived problems with the widely known church imaginary as people of God; among them, the relations between papal primacy and episcopal collegiality as well as between the universal and local church, the nature of lay and ordained ministry, and the church's evangelical and social mission.

Hinze's study reveals the impact of these developments on the church's ministry in dioceses and parishes. However, more fundamental than differences in theological perspectives of leaders is the impact on sensing the faith through these processes and structures. The inadequacy evident in how these processes and structures have been undertaken could undermine discerning the sense of the faith.[29]

This apparent inadequacy also provides the horizon of Baggett's earlier fieldwork, which consisted of participation in patronal feasts and liturgical celebrations and of conducting extensive surveys and interviews in six Bay Area parishes.[30] He relates all this data to the state of contemporary American Catholicism, which "has successfully negotiated the transition from a foreign church [brought by immigrants] to an American religious community"[31] and has of late experienced "divisions among the laity, as well as increasingly obvious discrepancies between their manner of being Catholic and church leaders' expectations."[32] This portrait shows commonly observed characteristics—shifting emphasis from the institutional to the personal, individual empowerment regarding belief and practice, and the diversity of views reflected in the so-called culture wars.

Taking this portrait as given, Baggett instead focuses on how these Catholics live and make sense of their faith, "a sense of how culture—in this case, Catholic culture—can be accessed, deployed, and improvised amid changing circumstances."[33] Noting the influence of the Vatican II teaching on conscience,[34] he describes his subjects' response to their situation as "defecting in place,"[35] so that they can disagree with particular church teachings and still be "a good Catholic."[36]

Thus "parishioners' negotiation with their religious tradition is both a rooting and an uprooting....As they take its symbols and meanings seriously while also negotiating them, they engender a different kind of Catholic self that is confronted by and attuned to the problems of the modern self more generally."[37]

Such defecting in place within church situations with inadequate structures for participation, however, does not necessarily lead to loss of hope in all parishioners nor to "'voting with their feet' and leaving."[38] Many value "their church communities as social spaces in which certain elements of the Catholic Church and American society can be both questioned and resisted"[39] and as "'sites of synchronized performance' whereby people jettison those aspects of themselves that seem less religious in order to engender a shared sense of the transcendence."[40] Moreover, the "traditionalist" and "progressive" sectors in these parishes share important communalities such as emphasizing inclusiveness, following tradition, and connecting to the broader church institution.[41]

According to Baggett, these sites of synchronized performance incarnate "the paradoxical nature of tradition," which is characterized by "three specific interpretative practices—negotiating, reframing, and innovating—through which Catholics have been instrumental in changing their religious tradition."[42]

From this perspective, Baggett's and Hinze's ethnographies portray a church that offers spaces for different and differing voices as well as processes and structures for participation and consultation. However, all these are imperfect because they prove vulnerable to competing internal and external forces and interests. Despite (or even because of) this imperfection, in both the Bay Area and New York parishes, many found their voices and expressed their concerns in stories told and concerted action—in Hinze's words, "laypeople, clergy, and bishops who continued to be inspired by the prophetic anointing that marks the church as people of God."[43]

In line with the theological understanding of sensing the faith, the sense of the faithful cannot be "reduced to acts of resistance to church authority on the part of a rebellious laity" or "a univocal assertion of lay interpretative authority, rather than a diversity of voices in dialogue, from laity, to theologians, to bishops."[44] Instead, "the primary measure…to assess the situation is to examine the vitality of the participatory structures dedicated to discerning the apostolic mission of the local church at the archdiocesan and parish levels"—in other words, asking how effective are the ecclesial processes and structures related to sensing the faith of the church?[45]

This gap between the theological account and actual practice is neither new nor unfamiliar to those engaged in pastoral ministry in whatever form. Nevertheless, they are often still inspired by the Vatican II image of the pilgrim church on the way to eschatological fulfillment and thus renew their commitment to continuing discernment of religious practice in terms of the faith of the church.

Sensing the Faith "From Below" and "At the Peripheries"

Given the gap between the theological account and the actual practice of sensing the faith, one cannot but recall the aggiornamento called for by Pope John XXIII. Cardinal Walter Kasper describes this "famous, though difficult to translate and often-abused word" thus: "It does not simply mean adapting to today, but the making of Tradition present today in its newness. Such 'renewal' is different from innovation. Renewal, rather, asserts the biblical understanding of 'new' in the sense of gracious, non-derivable, unused and continuously surprising eschatological newness."[46]

As described by Kasper and other recent writers, aggiornamento, with its related vocabulary of renewal and reform, has received greater currency upon Pope Francis's election. Thus, greater critical study and reflection have analyzed church reform in all its aspects and at every level. For instance, the 2015 international and multidisciplinary conference organized by the periodical *La Civiltá Cattolica* focused on "Reform(s) of and within the Church."[47] It explored the historical precedents, theological basis, and institutional ramifications of church reform—all with the view of supporting and facilitating aggiornamento characteristic of the synodal church on the way and promoted by Pope Francis's efforts at reform.

Within this general horizon of aggiornamento and in line with church programs for reform, bringing the actual practice of discerning about religious practices closer to the theological account of sensing the faith becomes crucial and urgent. Moreover, because institutional change management occurs through specific steps, there is a need for a strategic approach to guide the people of God in this discernment. This pastoral strategy for sensing the church's faith can be understood through two phrases, which, though distinct, are complementary and really belong to the same perspective. The phrases *from below* and *at the peripheries* have different genealogies and stress distinct nuances.

First, the strategic move to sense the faith "from below" is analogous to approaches first applied in Christology and, of late, ecclesiology. In these instances, "from below" and its counterpart "from above" are intended to "designate a point of departure and a method, not content."[48] Any approach from below, therefore, does not inevitably lead to forms of minimalism that diminish Jesus's divinity in Christology or bracket magisterial teaching in ecclesiology. On the contrary, "an ecclesiology from below cautions against reductionism in a historical and sociological interpretation of the church. The data for ecclesiology includes the empirical history of the genesis and development of the church and the development of the beliefs of the community about its nature and purpose. The church in its beginnings and constantly through its history bears witness to the presence and power of God in its origins, development, religious life, and future."[49]

In the context of such an ecclesiology, sensing the faith from below takes as its point of departure how Christians express their faith in everyday life, that is, in the lived Christianity that is integral to Christian tradition. This strategic approach to sensing the faith begins with and prioritizes how a particular religious practice expresses the communal and personal faith of those engaged in the practice.

In addition to having this point of departure, sensing the faith from below indicates a method that respects and reflects the symbolic and narrative nature of this religious practice. Inasmuch as Christians express their faith in diverse forms, many of which involve gesture and ritual or material objects and physical space, articulating the faith expressed must be done in relation to the faithful as historical subjects of tradition and to their wider social context rather than to narrow conceptual descriptions.

Second, sensing the faith "at the peripheries" is aligned with the "from below" approach but brings forth different dimensions, especially as elaborated in Pope Francis's statements. This vocabulary originates from multiple views in 1960s social science discourse—for instance, in Johan Galtung's Centre-Periphery Theory of Social Position and in dependency theories from Latin America and other nations in the Global South.[50] In many of these studies, center and periphery are sociogeographical sites that are linked but unequal in terms of economic and political power; hence, for the center, development takes place at the expense of the periphery's dependency, and for the peripheries, supposedly through "the trickle-down effect." Having been immersed in Latin American urban poor communities, Pope Francis is keenly aware of this asymmetrical relation in today's global order and has strongly condemned it in his writing.

But Pope Francis's distinct contribution to the understanding of peripheries and its significance for ecclesiology consists in its expanded meaning and application to the church. He does not limit peripheries to "a geo-political or geo-economic concept" but connects it "to the broader and deeper notions of exclusion, alienation, and expulsion."[51] Moreover, he applies this center-periphery perspective to the church itself. Before his election, he addressed cardinals at a preconclave meeting thus: "The Church is called to come out of herself and to go to the peripheries, not only geographically, but also the existential peripheries: the mystery of sin, of pain, of injustice, of ignorance and all forms of misery."[52] This call to the church is further elaborated in a subsequent papal interview:

> We must get out of ourselves and go toward the peripheries. We must avoid the spiritual disease of the Church that can become self-referential: when this happens, the Church itself becomes sick. It is true that accidents can happen when you go out into the street, as can happen to any man or woman. But if the Church remains closed onto itself; self-referential, it grows old. Between a Church that goes into the street and gets into an accident and a Church that is sick with self-referentiality, I have no doubts in preferring the first.[53]

This call to go to the peripheries carries significant ecclesiological import in sensing the faith of the church and discerning approbative reception of a particular religious practice. While it recalls the biblical prominence of the *anawim* or the recent terminology of "preferential option for the poor" and is deeply humanitarian in spirit, it addresses a more profound fundamental concern:

> I am convinced of one thing: the great changes in history were realized when reality was seen not from the center but rather from the peripheries. It is a hermeneutical question: reality is understood only if it is looked at from the peripheries, and not when our viewpoint is equidistant from everything. Truly to understand reality we need to move away from the central position of calmness and peacefulness and direct ourselves to the peripheral areas. Being at the peripheries helps to see and to understand better, to analyze reality more correctly, to shun centralism and ideological approaches.[54]

Here, one detects the formative influence on Pope Francis of the French Jesuit theologian Michel de Certeau.[55]

Put within an ecclesiological context, this bold statement indicates that the reality of the church itself is understood more faithfully when seen from the peripheries. Hence, sensing the faith from below and at the peripheries provides the hermeneutical key to the faith of God's people and Christ's disciples, and to the approbative reception of particular religious practices. It values the lived faith of Christian communities and individuals and pays keen attention to those at the peripheries.

Sensing the faith from below and at the peripheries offers both a point of departure and a method for the approbative reception of religious practices. Mindful of but not starting with theological articulations from the center, this pastoral strategic approach enters deeply into the lived Christianity of those at the peripheries, and from there explores whether these practices faithfully manifest the *sensus fidei* of God's people. Along the way, this approach could also suggest what reforms in the processes and structures of consultation and dialogue need to be undertaken.

This journey suggests what Walter Kasper describes in his recent volume on ecclesiology, the pilgrim church as "black but beautiful (Song 1:5)"—a biblical image appropriated by the church fathers possibly referring to a rustic sunburnt woman from outside the court but chosen by the king.[56] He explains it thus: "It is lovely, in spite of all its imperfections and wrinkles (Eph 5:27). It is of this beauty that I speak in this book to demonstrate how the Church can remain the one and the same Church of Jesus Christ and still not appear old. It can be new and young and can communicate to future generations what they need more than anything else: the hope that comes from faith."[57] Furthermore, "it [the Church] has often suffered inner crises and substantial scandals, but it has renewed itself again and up to the present it has produced uncountable holy men and women, who let themselves be consumed in the ministry for the poorest of the poor."[58]

Within the ambit of this church, the religious practice of those following Christ in their communal and personal lives derives its meaning as an integral part of Christian tradition through the work of the Spirit. As the pilgrim people of God, all its members—laity, theological community, and official teachers—listen to each other, especially to those at the peripheries, discerning faith expressions in religious practices and recognizing the sense of its faith.

PART IV

JOURNEYING WITH THE SHEEP

8

Theology and Sociology

IT WAS AT HIS FIRST Chrism Mass in 2013 when Pope Francis delivered his now famous line: "Be shepherds, with the 'smell of the sheep,' make it real, as shepherds among your flock."[1] Speaking before the clergy, Pope Francis made his heartfelt appeal for them to smell the sheep and to smell like sheep, now recurrent themes in his many statements. But what does Pope Francis mean? Writing the foreword for the pope's book, Bishop Robert Barron offers his reflections. To him, to smell the sheep and to smell like them is a call on pastors to be detached from material comfort and be readily available for their people. In doing so, they follow the Lord and find joy in him.

Our book began with this call, and we find it fitting to end with it. This final part presents our concluding remarks. Throughout the pages of this work, our attention to the theological sense and sociological significance of people's Christianity has been our way of living out this call. In lived religion, we find so much meaning that emanates from ordinary people's experiences. Given our respective disciplinal backgrounds, our interdisciplinary work has led us to recognize both the theological and sociological dimensions of people's Christianity. As we have explained throughout the book, God's engagement with humankind—both as individuals and as communities—involves all aspects of the human and the worldly. Thus, in approaching lived religion, our working premise is that God's presence embraces the fullness of human experience and social life. But as we have pointed out too, lived religion is not only about piety or rituals. As sociologists and anthropologists have demonstrated, devotional practices, prayers, and worship—even in the most mundane settings—are meaningful in their respective contexts.[2]

In many cases, these contexts are fraught with tensions that become the very content of devotional life. This is even far more acute for the disenfranchised, for whom community is about inclusion. Once again, the egalitarian character of the faith community is both theological and sociological. In such places as Tamil Nadu, where conversion to Catholicism has not led to any emancipation from the caste system, the "Catholic clergy speak the language of community in terms merely of moral unity and spiritual fraternity." But their statements hold "little meaning for the Dalit who experiences the bitter humiliations of physical and social separation both within and outside the church."[3]

And so, when pastors and observers turn their attention to the meanings that underpin religious practices, the call to build a community in which shepherds smell the sheep becomes undeniable and perhaps irresistible. No wonder Pope Francis, in the same message above, emphasizes that pastors need to "perceive in every request, even those requests that are inconvenient and at times purely material or downright banal—but only apparently so—the desire of our people to be anointed with fragrant oil."[4] To be a shepherd, therefore, is to exercise pastoral proximity and availability. But it also goes beyond that. That pastors embed themselves in the realities of their sheep provides them with access to contexts of inequality. For Emilce Cuda, this is the reason why Francis's role as a shepherd is also prophetic, for it entails the exercise of "the gift of prophecy as a denouncement of the true causes of injustice."[5] Significantly, this book has echoed multiple layers of the same call.

In this chapter, we wish to revisit the complex relationship between theology and sociology. We do this in a manner that reflects retrospectively on what we have tried to accomplish in this book. At the same time, we offer new ways of bringing the agenda forward. Inasmuch as our work has been on people's Christianity, the marriage between theology and sociology can offer new pathways for academic and pastoral work. Theology and sociology, after all, are distant disciplinal relatives whose relationship with each other has been replete with suspicion.[6] But when brought together in the spirit of collaboration, much can be accomplished. These disciplines offer practical insights for pastoral work and for the deepening of sociology insofar as its noble endeavors for social justice are concerned. We are moving from *lived* religion to *living* religion.

Specifically, we have three applications in mind. The first is the *sensus fidei*, which does not claim that the voice of the majority is the voice of truth. Beginning with the theological assumption that God guides us to discover God's ways, recent reflections on the *sensus fidei* are recognizing the input of sociological categories in making sense of contemporary faith. The second is *pastoral sociology*.[7] While it has progressed as a subfield in the West, its promise is only beginning to be discovered in many parts of the Global South. The third is *public theology*. The need for theology to engage public issues has been rendered far more urgent not by secularism but by the rise of populism and religious nationalism. Our hope is that by revisiting the thorny relationship between theology and sociology, we can inspire greater interdisciplinary work not just in seminaries but even in pastoral work.[8]

The Two Disciplines

Writing in 1915, Talbott defined theology as the "science of man's relation to God" and sociology as the "science of man's relation to his fellow-man."[9] In Talbott's worldview, there was no antagonism between these two disciplines. Calls both for social justice and the rediscovery of the prophetic tradition within the church made sense. This statement validates the early view that there was no inherent contradiction between sociology and theology. To be sure, Comte was convinced that sociology in nineteenth-century France was meant to replace religion. And yet in the United States, sociology emerged within Christian social reformism.[10] Elsewhere in Europe, what is now known as the International Society for the Study of Religion began as the International Conference of Religious Sociology.[11] The hostility between the two disciplines is thus arguably a recent development.

Indeed, the situation today is much different, if only because both disciplines have become hostile to each other. The tension is not only due to their specific objects of study. Their orientations have become far more distinct. While theology is normative, sociology is empirical.[12] The tension is inherent in their competing claims to truth, of which intellectual origin is found in the Enlightenment, during which theology, as "valid knowledge," was called into question.[13] For a sociologist, a sacrament such as baptism might be a rite of passage comparable to rituals in other cultures or religious traditions. But to a theologian, its metaphysical merits are revolutionary.[14] While religion is theology's habitation, for sociology it is its object of study.

Thus, academics from both sides of the aisle suspect each other of malice and hostility toward their own methods and claims. Fr. Andrew Greeley's observation is astute, if not blunt: "Theologians who are concerned almost to the point of obsession with the proper methodology for their own discipline seem to consider themselves dispensed from the methodologies of those disciplines that observe and analyze society when they, the theologians, want to discuss society."[15] Such degree of resistance is evident, too, in sociology: "The properties theology embodies, of myth, magic, and superstition, straddle the relationships of sociology with anthropology. If admitted to sociology, they belong to issues of ethnography and exotic cultures."[16] Such hostility is the result of a long history of disciplinal differentiation that began with the Enlightenment, a separation that classical sociologists have rendered almost irrevocable by anticipating the decline of religion.[17] Furthermore, sociology has been accused of the "usurpation and secularization of the gospel" for offering a salvation story devoid of Christian narratives.[18]

And yet to revisit the link, as this section will demonstrate, has become a welcome development for sympathetic scholars on both sides of the aisle. This is a recent development that has yet to gain traction in mainstream theology and the social sciences. Nevertheless, the openness is a recognition among theologians that other disciplines are worth engaging for the insights they provide about the world and social reality. Thus, theology has bravely interfaced with developments in the social sciences such as Marxism, feminism, and postmodernism. "Underlying all these engagements," according to Filipino Vincentian priest Danilo Pilario, "is the belief that if theology is 'faith seeking understanding,' such 'understanding' cannot be a monopoly of the revealed word; it can *also* be discerned in the frameworks of contemporary sciences. Or, better still, the Word itself can *only* be revealed in the power and fragility of human reason."[19]

THE VALUE OF SOCIOLOGY IN THEOLOGY

Some scholarship has been devoted to the value of sociology in theological thinking. In biblical studies, for example, its main contribution has been in deciphering the social and cultural contexts in order to understand the meaning of scriptural texts.[20] In this section, however, we want to focus on the value of sociology in theologizing people's Christianity. Specifically, its value is not in questioning the metaphysics that underlie lived religion but in assessing its transformations in contemporary society. Much of the recent reflections about religion and the marketization of society may be applied in this manner.[21] Another example is the very trajectory of the study of popular religion as a "turn to everyday authenticity," which parallels the transformations within lived religion itself.[22] Indeed, at the heart of the sociology of religion is its interest in religious change, which accompanies social transformation. The most common is secularization, which renders institutional religion irrelevant. It is, however, more acute in the Global North than it is elsewhere. Around the world, there are many other religious trends worth investigating, including the rise of alternative spiritualities and traditions.[23]

The other value of sociology is in locating theological worldviews that underpin people's Christianity in concrete contexts. Sociology can ground theology, as it were. If lived religion in the form of rituals, processions, and practices is about enabling people to navigate from the seen to the unseen, then what else might fulfill this task in societies in which religious change is taking place? The answer, Flanagan argues in a provocative work, lies in turning to sociology as one reflects on religious endeavors: "Dealing with the paradoxes of the seen and the unseen are matters proper to theology, for they involve eyes of faith, but they also embody ways of seeing that are culturally contingent."[24] It might be essential for sociology to make a leap of faith to theology if only to have a grasp of people's motivations that underpin their lived religion.

Inspired by Simmel's writings about people's beliefs in God and their behavior toward one another, Flanagan also asserts that "pushing sociology into theology permits it to ask questions of those for whom a leap of faith is acceptable for the sense of the ultimate it can realize, when everything else in culture seems senseless."[25] Indeed, in an earlier writing, he claims that one's analytical approach can begin with the interior yearning of the self toward the transcendent, based on which one can make sense of the individual's religious beliefs and practices. In other words, "the social is a means through which the individual fulfills desires to find compass points upon which belief can be realized and recognized."[26] This point strongly echoes Andrew Greeley's work on religious sensibility, which refers to how people make sense of their lived religion based on experience and intellectual reflection. The call, therefore, is for scholars and observers to be open to the religious sensibilities that underpin lived religion, the very premise of our book.

Finally, thinking about how sociology grounds theology offers a critical edge to discern power relations in lived religion. Conflict stemming from religious divisions is an example. For David Martin, sociology offers the tools to approach religious and social problems since "much that happens by way of divisions between churches or by way of violence between Christian peoples or through violence in general can be seen as deeply embedded in social nature and process."[27] Theology, as a discursive exercise, has material contexts, and recent theological writings are now beginning to ask whether it is also consequential.[28] Religious nationalism, for example, is grounded in theological worldviews that manifest themselves in political choices.[29] In the Philippines, theological nationalism accounts for the resistance toward any progressive policy related to sexuality, divorce, or reproductive health.[30] Power relations also characterize theological discourse. What counts as theologically valid is often a result of contestations not just within the hierarchy but even in local congregations and parishes. They are "fields of power struggles" or "sites of contested meaning-making where prophetic voices, though often silenced, can emerge."[31] This is a sociological insight that sheds light on how listening even to the minority is tied to the *sensus fidei*, a point to which we will return.

SOCIOLOGY AS THEOLOGY

Although theology has extended an olive branch to the social sciences, the latter does not typically reciprocate the favor. This continues to be the dominant attitude in the social sciences especially in universities, for example, where theology departments need to justify their existence by evolving into a more acceptable version in the form of religious studies.[32] Some intellectual reflexivity is necessary here. Perhaps the distance between sociology and theology is not as wide as it has been portrayed in scholarship. In recent years, a few sociologists have begun reflecting on the very theological underpinnings of their discipline. Compared to theology, this seems to be a late development, especially when one considers how open the former has become to other disciplines in reflecting on human existence and contemporary issues. With much reflexivity, theology entertains developments in the natural and social sciences. And yet other disciplines have kept a distance from theology.

In a provocative work, Christian Smith turns the tables on his fellow sociologists, arguing that despite their discipline's secularism, it is in fact very much driven by sacred pursuits.[33] Inherent to sociology, in other words, is a theological worldview. Its pursuits are not necessarily transcendental but are directly related to compelling humanistic principles for the sake of emancipation. The emancipatory project draws inspiration from different intellectual sources, including liberal individualism, Marxism, and progressive social reform. For Smith, sociology—at least the American variant—is committed to the "emancipation, equality, and moral affirmation of all human beings as autonomous, self-directing, individual agents (who should be) out to live their lives as they personally so desire, by constructing their own favored identities, entering and exiting relationships as they choose, and equally enjoying the gratification of experiential, material, and bodily pleasures."[34]

The project is neither programmatic nor monolithic. Instead, the commitment frames the guiding principles that shape curriculum, training, and initiatives. In other words, even if sociology might be functionally atheistic, at the very least, it embraces sacred principles. At a closer look, the emancipatory drive of the social sciences, from psychology to sociology, very much reflects the salvific narrative of Christianity. What exorcism is to possession, therapy is to personal troubles. The same can be said about analysis and efforts at social liberation from class struggle.[35]

The theological dimension is also evident in some of the assumptions of sociological inquiry and writings. When social scientists wrote about the Holocaust, they resorted to religious language to capture the evil of its atrocities. Writing in the early twentieth century, Dietrich Bonhoeffer's work is as much sociological as it is theological. For him, social relationships are possible because the human being can transcend the self toward the other, a sociological moment that mirrors the relational ethos of the divine.[36] Along similar lines, the postmodern condition raises crucial questions about what it means to be human. Therefore, the interest in human relationships and in what could sustain them at a time when they have become ephemeral, unstable, and liquid recurs.[37]

Smelling the Sheep and the Sociological Enterprise

One important lesson about pursuing interdisciplinary work between theology and sociology and the social sciences at large is that one cannot be subsumed to the other. This is because each discipline has its own methodological and ontological inadequacies. The point of interdisciplinary work is to draw on each other's analytical strengths. For James Sweeney, sociology and theology pay attention to different "raw data": "The primordial form of knowing that theology works with is belief, whereas sociology works with our regular, ordinary, 'common sense' knowledge of the world. The task, in both cases, is to systematise and thematise and refine the raw data as theory—sociological and theological."[38]

Consequently, any discipline is not simply a "handmaid of theology." In a manner of speaking, the task of theology is to find moments or sites of grace in the sociological. Adopting this line of thinking also entails consciously adopting an analytically open attitude among both theologians and social scientists. To this end, speaking a common language of faith is beneficial. But more importantly, interdisciplinary work demands recognition of the epistemological merits of both disciplines. Doing so is necessary in avoiding condemnatory dispositions toward the findings and claims of each discipline.

This is the same attitude that we have embraced as a theologian and as a sociologist in writing this book. Our point of origin is that popular religion, often derided, is a site of both theological and sociological reflection. As the previous chapters have shown, places where depth of faith and aspirations for social liberation coexist are examples of lived religion or what we refer to as people's Christianity. In the following sections, we present three areas in which greater interdisciplinary work is needed with respect to people's Christianity: the *sensus fidei*, pastoral sociology, and public theology.

SENSUS FIDEI

The theological premise of *sensus fidei* is that the whole people of God have been gifted with an ability to discern convictions, morals, and other matters of faith. The *people of God*, it is important to note, does not only refer to the laity. Everyone in the church has this gift of discernment for the "deepening of the understanding of the faith and of the praxis of the faith."[39] In other words, the Spirit of God is at work to empower his people "to live their lives in pursuit of and in accord with Christian truth as they inhabit it."[40] Inspired by Pope Francis's openness to cultural diversity inherent in the people of God, Burkhard makes the case for divine revelation as a dynamic mechanism that engages personal and communal experience for divine revelation to be fully grasped by believers. In this sense, the *sensus fidei* is a communicative moment between God's self-revelation and human response.

The *sensus fidei* noticeably banks on the radical equality among all the baptized. Therefore, while there is a communal dimension to *sensus fidei*, there is also an individual dimension. Individuals have the capacity to receive God's self-revelation, which they make sense of in the context of their own experiences. In making sense of God's self-revelation, individuals look to Christ as the norm and their lives as the form: "If the norm of a faithful *sensus fidei* is Jesus Christ as witnessed to in Scripture and tradition, then the primary form of a *sensus fidei* is a life lived out in fidelity to Jesus Christ within the community of the Church."[41] Thus, theological reflections derived from the *sensus fidei* ought to bring hope.[42]

Consequently, there is so much to be gleaned from lived religion as a *locus theologicus*. At one level, lived religion is where God's self-revelation, invoking religious narratives and symbols, manifests itself. At another level, lived religion is also the individual and communal response to God's work in human experience. In the previous chapters, we characterized popular devotion as acts of gratitude or even expressions of never-ending commitment to the work of God. Therefore, lived religion is people's Christianity. To be sure, clerical resistance to popular piety still recurs, especially when it occurs in rivalry with the official liturgy of the church. But recent theological developments, drawing from Vatican II, are recognizing the value of people's Christianity.[43] One reflection in this regard is that lived religion demonstrates how the people of God are responding to divine revelation in ways that deepen their faith and practice of it. In *Evangelii Gaudium*, Pope Francis makes the following case about popular religion:

> Underlying popular piety, as a fruit of the inculturated Gospel, is an active evangelizing power which we must not underestimate: to do so would be to fail to recognize the work of the Holy Spirit. Instead, we are called to promote and strengthen it, in order to deepen the never-ending process of inculturation. Expressions of popular piety have much to teach us; for those who are capable of reading them, they are a *locus theologicus* which demands our attention, especially at a time when we are looking to the new evangelization. (no. 126)

Certainly, the sociological input is necessary in appreciating how lived religion emerges out of specific social, historical, and cultural contexts. As discussed in chapter 4, popular practices such as communal prayer can have emancipatory aspirations for marginalized people and groups. Much of these social aspirations couched in religious language is accessible, for example, via the content of their prayers.[44] Assertions about their devotional practice are also useful in recognizing the everyday theology at work.[45] But as a way forward for scholarly and pastoral inquiry, it might be useful to consider what is left unsaid. Baggett refers to this sociological approach as being "absence-minded."[46] What might remain unstated reveals significant information about how ordinary people situate themselves in relation to the religious hierarchy, their own congregation, or institutional theology. To be "absence-minded" is essential in discerning the influence of local culture and broader societal trends such as religious subjectivization on what it means to believe in and practice the Christian faith.

Moreover, being absence-minded calls for a deliberate inclusion of those who are marginalized—those who are deliberately excluded from theological conversations. It is "in the midst of the concrete realities of daily life that marginalized people, individually and communally, experience revelation and encounter God. It is where sin, as well as compassion and grace, is experienced."[47] While the *sensus fidelium*—sense of the faithful—is a collective effort on the part of clergy, theologians, and the laity, there is wisdom in beginning from the margins. It is a starting point if theological reflections were to make Christ and the hope that he brings a lived reality. This is why drawing on social scientific methods to describe what ordinary believers adhere to is simply inadequate.[48] Indeed, in engaging those who are marginalized—or smelling the sheep—"we could talk amongst other things about the biases, silences, and lacunae in the theological examination of devotion, the relationship between faith lived and faith discussed, and the role of the Holy Spirit in the unexpected."[49]

We offer a final note about including those who are marginalized. To do so demands a critical attitude on the part of scholars and pastoral workers. Despite the egalitarian character of the people of God, the hierarchical nature of institutional Christianity asserts the authority of the clergy. Clericalism partly accounts for it. But the problem has been exacerbated by the power struggle, even at the level of congregations and parishes, that may leave ordinary believers disillusioned.[50] To be "conflict-minded" is to be cognizant of how dissent or alternative voices are deliberately silenced at every level of the institution.[51]

PASTORAL SOCIOLOGY

The second area in which greater interdisciplinary work between theology and the social sciences must be pursued is pastoral sociology. Pastoral sociology is the "integration of social science methods, theory, and research findings with the theological language and self-understanding of church life and ministry."[52] The sociological input is inescapable because all pastoral work relates to institutions and social structures.[53] With this understanding, pastoral sociology is inherently interdisciplinary. It is, essentially, a subfield of both practical theology and applied social science.

Pastoral sociology first emerged in Europe in the 1940s. Working within the framework of churches, sociologists of religion provided empirical assessments of the social contexts immediately after the war.[54] At that time, Protestants in Western Europe were setting up research institutes and conducting research on such topics as secularization. In the 1960s, it gained prominence in the Catholic Church when Vatican II called for the establishment of institutes of pastoral sociology to assist apostolates around the world. According to *Christus Dominus*, ministerial work "should be properly adapted to the needs of the present day with regard not only for man's spiritual and moral circumstances but also for his social, demographic, and economic conditions" (no. 17).[55] The document asserts that "religious and social research, through offices of pastoral sociology, contributes much to the efficacious and fruitful attainment of that goal" (no. 17).

Inspired by this call, pastoral sociologists became preoccupied with different interests over the twentieth century. In North America, their concerns revolved around parish life, religious vocation, and social justice. At the turn of the century, pastoral planning needed sociological insights as dioceses had to confront decline in personnel. Despite the decline, however, opportunities for new faith communities that are more horizontal emerged within the Catholic Church.[56] In Western Europe, religious decline was also the backdrop against which pastoral sociology operated. The situation was unexpected as churches anticipated religious resurgence after the war. Changing sexual practices also indicated that religious institutions were out of touch with reality.[57]

Pastoral sociology, therefore, must begin to entertain lived religion as a site for both theological reflections and pastoral care. This is because there is so much to be understood about the religious identities, beliefs, and worldviews that underpin lived religion. In asserting this point, we take inspiration from recent developments in pastoral theology that recognize communities as "creators of culture in a theological idiom."[58]

The wide methodological arsenal of the social sciences is helpful in discovering these theological idioms. The biographical or narrative approach, for example, allows individuals to explain their life stories, which then become the backdrop to their lived religion. These narratives not only disclose the experiences that account for their religious practices, but they also reveal faith journeys, transformations, and aspirations about the future.[59] Having a broad overview of personal and communal faith journeys can provide significant information about what pastoral interventions are timely and appropriate. Furthermore, ethnographic work is useful in making sense of religious practices. Illnesses, for example, point to the creative work of lived religion in making God's presence felt in the lives of the suffering. Dunlap's work shows that congregations may have different theological explanations for illnesses, but their prayers, confessions, acts of compassion, and even greeting cards are creative ways of negotiating the finitude of the human body and inadequacy of health care.[60] Recognizing these negotiations fosters empathy in pastoral care and encourages ministers to creatively draw on material religion and everyday beliefs in expressing it.

Using sociological methods, pastoral sociology can also provide critical assessments of pastoral care. In fact, pastoral theologians themselves have been at the forefront of such assessments. Their work includes the "observation of the role of particular theological truth claims, for good or ill, in the practices of actual communities."[61] For example, the preoccupation with spiritual warfare among ministers and ordinary believers makes it difficult for them to provide sound diagnosis and care with respect to mental conditions.[62] Moreover, organizational structures have led to the unintended consequence of creating more obstacles instead of fostering more opportunities for people's participation in religious communities. A critical approach can identify the social factors behind community disempowerment such as the leadership qualities of priests and hierarchical structures. In Brazil, for example, the establishment of local councils to police "proper ritual" has "undermined the autonomy of grassroots initiatives" among Base Christian Communities.[63]

Despite its empirical orientation, pastoral sociology provides very useful analytical frameworks to reflect theologically about lived religion. Perhaps the most evident is the idea that the self is formed in the context of human relationships. How people understand themselves, behave accordingly, and relate to others is an ongoing process that keeps transforming as new interactions emerge. Although this idea is basic in sociology, its roots are arguably older, to be found in the relational character of the Trinity.[64] This parallelism opens many opportunities to make sense of lived religion as a way to relate to God and also to relate to other fellow human beings. Amid this relational act, one becomes transformed—a process that is both sociological and theological. Finally, this theological reading reveals the inadequacy of relying only on the directly observable and measurable. It has been a criticism of pastoral sociology since it emerged in the 1940s. Underlying the measurable is the immeasurable, or what Ziemann, citing Luckmann, refers to as the invisible religion, the "smaller patterns of transcendence that cannot be conceptualised by the means of church sociography."[65] In the context of lived religion, much of which cannot be measured, sociological reflexivity is as indispensable as theological perceptiveness.

PUBLIC THEOLOGY

The last area of interdisciplinary work is public theology. The dominant understanding about public theology is that it is mainly a theological commentary on social and political issues using publicly accessible reason. Its main task is to offer a Christian perspective on public matters, usually following the principles of the common good. In doing so, public theology engages different bodies of the public sphere, including civil society, academe, media, market, the state, and other religious groups. Sebastian Kim's accessible work lists the norms of doing public theology as it engages the public sphere. Some of these norms include:

- witnessing to Christian values for the sake of the common good;
- articulating these ideas in a manner accessible to people outside the faith;
- relating public debates to the Christian tradition for those in congregations;
- being thoroughly familiar with issues and policies at stake to assess them analytically and theologically;
- giving preference to the voices of victims and survivors for the sake of justice;
- requiring theology to engage other disciplines.[66]

But public theology has so much potential when applied in the context of lived religion. We propose this point having been inspired by the work of Miller-McLemore to redefine pastoral theology as public theology. In the context of the United States, two main concerns underpin the call.[67] The first is the inability of Christianity, for one reason or another, to comment on social issues. The second is the inadequacy of pastoral work's focus on the individual alone. Although these concerns are situated in the United States, they are highly applicable to many contexts around the world, especially in places where Christianity is focused solely on individualistic concerns such as salvation, prosperity, and well-being.

What is the shape of public theology when applied in the context of lived religion? Several possibilities are available depending on how one approaches public theology. Some scholars have pushed for the adoption of a christological framework that embraces egalitarianism and hope whenever churches and ordinary believers reflect on policies and social issues.[68] Consequently, public theology is not about asserting a point in a condescending manner, nor is it about employing a sophisticated language that excludes other people from being engaged in deliberation with one another. This point seems basic, but as Wustmans notes, public engagements made by intellectuals—religious included—tend to be one-directional.[69] Bringing to the surface the participatory, egalitarian, and hopeful model of lived religion can provide viable alternatives to the rise of authoritarian regimes in contemporary global society. Lived religion as communal initiatives presents itself as an alternative form of solidarity where public theology can flourish. We take inspiration from reflections about community organizing as a praxis of public theology. Community organizing can "unmask, fight against, and bring accountability to concentrations of economic and political power that over-determine and dominate our common life."[70]

Other scholars build on this latter point. For them, public theology needs to be praxis-oriented, which emphasizes the role of church and civil society in working for the common good.[71] This is a promising line of thinking that resurrects the collective spirit that pervades lived religion. Although lived religion can also be hierarchical, much of it is very egalitarian and organic—and, as we have noted, can be arrested by ill-advised pastoral work and imposed organizational structure.[72] The egalitarian nature of public theology provides a method for both the sociological and theological disciplines to reflect on the issues that confront religious communities. Everyday religious rituals, for example, provide the moral framework for believers to understand and respond to the issues confronting them. Breaking bread at a common table and making the sign of peace toward one another are in themselves the theological language by which communities can galvanize solidarity and critique inequality.[73] Beyond the ritual, cases also abound. Religious communities are organizing themselves to respond directly to local concerns. Basic ecclesial communities, for example, are working for participatory sustainable development in areas that big business interests are taking over.[74] In partnership with religious leaders, these church communities are critiquing neoliberal policies in the light of faith. Lived religion, in this sense, goes against the grain of the marketization of society and the privatization of faith.[75]

Finally, some scholars are also pushing the boundaries of public theology by recognizing its diverse sources. For the most part, the impression is that theologians or believers who wish to have an impact on public issues dominate public theology. Consequently, there is the view that public theology is "Christians engaging in dialogue with those outside church circles on various issues of common interest."[76] The impression is understandable given the origins of public theology in theological circles. In a pluralistic society, however, religious echoes are to be found in every sphere, including art, music, and popular culture. Therefore, scholars are now paying attention to the "reflective and critical talk about God in the public realm of our secular culture through arts, literature, cinema, theatre, music, as well as politics."[77] This is another point that points to the interdisciplinary work expected of public theology. It relies on the social sciences not only to make sense of contemporary social issues but also to discern the spaces in which religious ideas are echoed. In the same spirit, lived religion might be evident in nontraditional settings. As we have pointed out in previous chapters, lived religion is often a hybrid and even draws on popular culture.[78] To do a public theology of lived religion—taken in a broad sense—is a stimulating feat that questions how ordinary people in different spheres are drawing on religious resources to reflect on contemporary issues.

To employ public theology in lived religion also demands a critical attitude. This is in keeping with the call for honest assessments of theology in public life.[79] Inasmuch as public theology embraces principles of the common good, what it means and how it affects communities on the ground vary. For Meireis and Schieder, therefore, an effort must be made to "explore and critically reflect on the public impact of a polyphonic religious discourse and the religious dimension of public discourse."[80] To do so is urgent given the rise of religious nationalism and militant Christianity that feeds into the public support for populist regimes.[81]

Conclusion

We began this chapter (and this book) with Pope Francis's image addressed to pastors about smelling the sheep and thus smelling like sheep. Drawing from sociological analysis and theological reflection, we argued that this call entails foregrounding lived Christianity and considering how the *sensus fidei*, pastoral sociology, and public theology are viable ways of taking advantage of the synergy between theology and sociology.

On a final note, the image based on smelling is exceptional because it uses our olfactory sense to describe a pastoral-theological imperative. Among our senses, smell is rarely used for this purpose. De Guzman's recent essay, "The Scent of Marginality: Odorizing Difference in Migratory Relations," is an exception.[82] More often employed is the sense of sight; for instance, as noted in chapter 7, patristic writers and contemporary theologians speak of "the eyes of faith" with which we see our relations with God, the world, and each other.

And yet, the *sensus fidei*, pastoral sociology, and public theology appear more akin to our sense of smell than to that of sight. With our eyes, we either see or do not, and what we perceive is a unified picture, even when its definition is not crystal clear. Thus, we run the risk of understanding faith in terms of black or white, seeing or not seeing, as some theologians have done. By contrast, smelling the faith puts greater emphasis on breathing it all in, as it were. The metaphor is compelling and points to the transformative character of the process. Indeed, it is impossible to smell the sheep without eventually smelling like them. We take this further in our concluding chapter, in which we consider another image from Pope Francis—of the church as *synodos*, journeying together—not coincidentally, the theme of the October 2022 Synod of Bishops. The relation between these images is not only organic but also progressive.

9

From Smelling like Sheep to Journeying Together

IN PART 3, we discussed how lived religion in general and popular practice in particular is inherent to Christian tradition and is therefore the fundamental *locus theologicus*, the space in which shepherd and sheep sense divine presence unfolding in the world. At one level, lived religion is where God's self-revelation manifests itself through religious narratives and symbols. At another level, lived religion is also where individual and church respond to this work of the Spirit in human experience.

This significance of people's Christianity, recognized in recent theological reflection based on Vatican II,[1] is further affirmed in Pope Francis's first exhortation, *Evangelii Gaudium*:

> Underlying popular piety, as a fruit of the inculturated Gospel, is an active evangelizing power which we must not underestimate: to do so would be to fail to recognize the work of the Holy Spirit. Instead, we are called to promote and strengthen it, in order to deepen the never-ending process of inculturation. Expressions of popular piety have much to teach us; for those who are capable of reading them, they are a *locus theologicus* which demands our attention,

> especially at a time when we are looking to the new evangelization. (no. 126)

Hence lived Christianity is nothing less than the sacred space for the *sensus fidei*, for smelling the faith, so to speak.

The previous chapter ended with a note on the transformative character of smelling the sheep. Indeed, this has been the motif of our entire book. But our final chapter takes it one step further. We draw on another image from Pope Francis—as *synodos*, the people of God journeying together. As we have noted, the relation between these two images is not only organic but also progressive. After all, proximity and availability—practical applications of the call to smell the sheep—are about being present with and for one another.

Smelling the Faith

The image of smelling the faith captures the theological meaning of the *sensus fidei* (see chapters 7 and 8). In the image, one finds the dynamic characteristic of the *sensus fidei* as *organon*. The people of God receive this *organon* to smell the faith—this gift of discernment for the "deepening of the understanding of the faith and of the praxis of the faith."[2] They are empowered by God's Spirit "to live their lives in pursuit of and in accord with Christian truth as they inhabit it" and thus to discern convictions, morals, and other matters of faith.[3]

Because of the fundamental equality of the baptized, this gift to discern is common to and shared by God's people in all their diversity. Given this capacity that is neither hypothetical nor indeterminate but oriented toward faith, shepherd and sheep alike share their sensing of the faith with each other. They sharpen their sense of and for the faith to recognize, discover, and receive authentic expressions of faith as a response to God's self-revelation within Christian tradition.

As we noted in the previous chapter, this dynamic of sensing the faith engenders articulation and reception of the church's authentic faith: "If the norm of a faithful *sensus fidei* is Jesus Christ as witnessed to in Scripture and tradition, then the primary form of a *sensus fidei* is a life lived out in fidelity to Jesus Christ within the community of the Church."[4]

This integration of norm and form finds articulation as *sensus fidelium* in the texts of tradition as well as in the lives of faith of all the baptized. But since these texts never capture the full mystery of God's self-disclosure and the total authenticity of faith, these articulations, even those official, remain open to more precision, better expression, or even revision. As the long history of the church attests, sensing the faith is inherently an ongoing dynamic this side of history.

Given this enduring historical dynamic of smelling the faith, our sociological explorations have sharpened our sense of its unfolding. We have underscored how lived religion emerges out of specific social, historical, and cultural contexts and expresses the people's everyday theology at work.[5] For example, chapter 4 pointed to popular practices such as communal prayer possessing emancipatory aspirations couched in religious language,[6] and chapter 6 to Marian devotions evoking the human dialogue with God in complex sociological and theological dynamics. Our second chapter situated these examples in the context of lived Christianity around the world.

These explorations, therefore, have revealed the experiential and empirical unfolding of the *sensus fidei*. Whether in such popular devotions as the Black Nazarene procession in Manila or in the local ecclesial experiences of New York parishes, they uncover the tortuous process of smelling the faith. Clerical resistance to popular piety, acknowledged by the Vatican *Directory* discussed in chapter 3, is made visible. The implementation of structures for consulting the faithful mentioned in the 2014 ITC document on *sensus fidei* often failed to deliver.

Journeying Together

Through these imperfections, however, we see that the dynamic thrust of the *sensus fidei* remains, even intensifies, in the call for aggiornamento on all fronts, for instance, in Pope Francis's persistent call to embrace those at the peripheries, because it is "in the midst of the concrete realities of daily life that marginal(ized) people, individually and communally, experience revelation and encounter God. It is where sin is experienced as well as compassion and grace."[7] In smelling the least among the sheep, "we could talk amongst other things about the biases, silences, and lacunae in the theological examination of devotion, the relationship between faith lived and faith discussed, and the role of the Holy Spirit in the unexpected."[8]

This ever-present and never-completed dynamic of the *sensus fidei* through changing times and diverse places, represented in the image of smelling the sheep, leads to Pope Francis's second image of journeying together, associated with our bodily sense of motion and articulated theologically as "synodality." Although this image is borrowed from Vatican II and is implicit but operative in Scripture, tradition, and history,[9] he places it center stage, making it "permeate the key moments of the pontificate: the Bishop's Synod of 2014–15 on the family and marriage, the Synod of 2018 on the youth, and the Synod of 2019 for the Amazon region, but also Francis' understanding of the ordinary and extraordinary governance of the Church, and of the new kind of relationship between center and periphery, between clergy and laity, between different Catholic churches in the global Church."[10] Moreover, these moments are memorialized in his major works, *Evangelii Gaudium* (2013), *Laudato Si'* (2015), and *Amoris Laetitia* (2016), among others, and not surprisingly, in the theme of the Synod of 2022, "For a Synodal Church: Communion, Participation and Mission."

DYNAMISM

The first quality found in both images and indicative of their integral relation is the manifest dynamic character of the *sensus fidei* and the ecclesial journey, which undermine notions of faith and church in static essentialist terms. Smelling the faith in the sheep is a vibrant and challenging process of discernment within and through the lived Christianity of the faithful. This same dynamic characterizes the journey of the people of God throughout history.

In both instances, this unfolding dynamic is neither blind without destination nor meandering without promise, as the Israelites felt in the desert. Through the knotted processes that individual believers and the church in community undertake in sensing the faith and moving in hope, the guiding hand of the Spirit remains constant. Just as the *organon* for and orientation of the *sensus fidei* are God-given, a synodal church, to paraphrase Pope Francis, "allow[s] for shared discernment of the Holy Spirit, so that all may truly 'journey together,' led by the Spirit in living the church's faith and mission within history and with eschatological hope."[11]

This points to the integral relation of the two images, since the discernment involved in both moves toward greater authenticity in the church's faith and closer following of the way of Jesus. Its goal then is "not to discern whether other persons are holy or good and so are therefore trustworthy mediators of the church's tradition....Discernment in this sense is a synodal practice because it is a practice of discipleship, a means of learning how Christ lives within and calls forth believers and their communities, making them the faithful pilgrim people of God."[12] Thus sensing the faith is also an eschatological pilgrimage.

COMMUNITY

The other quality shared by these images charts the progression from the first to the other. As noted in chapter 7, the 2014 ITC document clearly affirms that sensing the faith is undertaken in community and requires the attitude of trust and the practice of consultation involving all the faithful.

However, Pope Francis's description of the image of journeying together not only draws practical implications but, more importantly, moves toward fresh pastures. While remaining in continuity with tradition, it stresses the quality of relatedness in ecclesial discernment. In short, Pope Francis asks, "How do the People of God journey *together* without losing their way?"

In his historic speech commemorating the fiftieth anniversary of the institution of the Synod of Bishops, he describes relations within the church in terms of an inverted pyramid: "In this Church, as in an inverted pyramid, the top is located beneath the base. Consequently, those who exercise authority are called 'ministers,' because, in the original meaning of the word, they are the least of all. It is in serving the people of God that each bishop becomes, for that portion of the flock entrusted to him, *vicarius Christi*, the vicar of that Jesus who at the Last Supper bent down to wash the feet of the Apostles (cf. John 13:1–15)."[13]

For Pope Francis, then, journeying together calls for "a Church which listens, which realizes that listening 'is more than simply hearing.' It is a mutual listening in which everyone has something to learn. The faithful people, the college of bishops, the Bishop of Rome: all listening to each other, and all listening to the Holy Spirit, the 'Spirit of truth' (*Jn* 14:17), in order to know what he 'says to the Churches' (*Rev* 2:7)."[14]

This qualifies the very nature of relations within the church. While the 2014 ITC document on the *sensus fidei* describes this in terms of consulting the faithful, *Evangelii Gaudium* underscores mutuality: "If we really believe in the abundantly free working of the Holy Spirit, we can learn so much from one another! It is not just about being better informed about others, but rather about reaping what the Spirit has sown in them, which is also meant to be a gift to us" (no. 246). This mutuality strives toward authentic consensus, which "requires the honest sharing of the sense of faith lived within diverse and intersecting contexts: geographical, historical, cultural, racial, political, and economic. It is through and in relationship to these contexts that the church journeys within history."[15]

Additionally, journeying together calls for space that protects and nourishes these relations, as "the essence of synodality itself dictates that in order to journey together, the People of God must come together to identify and commit to practices, structures, and methodologies which allow for mutual listening, discernment, and decision-making."[16]

Recent official documents have heeded this call, including the section "Ways of Consulting the Faithful" in the 2014 document on the *sensus fidei*, and the more extensive chapter 3 "Implementing Synodality" of the 2018 document on Synodality (*Sensus Fidei* 120–26).[17]

But more than in these texts, the image of the people of God journeying together comes alive in Pope Francis's way of proceeding, particularly in and through the synods he has convened. Their preparation, conduct, and documentation have been steps in journeying together—for instance, in gathering many voices, preparing the agenda, and allowing debate during sessions. He has even legislated changes in synodal procedures through his apostolic constitution *Episcopalis Communio* (Episcopal Communion) of September 15, 2018.

Indeed, the image of journeying together has become a constant theme in Pope Francis's words and actions and has provided solid theological ground and greater pastoral space for smelling the faith in the lived Christianity of God's People: "Francis' pontificate, his theological emphasis, and his experience of synodality is clearly at the beginning of a new path for the Catholic Church which he acknowledged since his first document, *Evangelii Gaudium*, when he wrote about the '*infallibilitas in credendo*' (*EG* 119) of the People of God,"[18] and "it is necessary to take distance from a static understanding of *consensus fidelium*, understood only as a unanimity in a given expression of faith."[19]

Conclusion

While the first image of smelling the sheep was addressed to church pastors, the second image calls the entire people of God to journey together in faith. Sensing the faith by smelling like sheep participates in the Spirit-driven dynamic behind the church's pilgrimage: "If synodality is, as Pope Francis has claimed, constitutive of the church, then this shared pilgrimage is the Holy Spirit's gift to the church. And yet this gift also calls the church to fulfill its mission through discernment of the *sensus fidelium*, developing synodal methodologies, and receiving ecumenical gifts."[20]

Though these images and their articulation from Pope Francis have brought some fresh air, they have received commendation and critique in vibrant and sometimes contentious popular and scholarly discussions. We need further explorations of the theological relation between synodality and collegiality as well as the existing pastoral situations within local churches and in the global context.

But given where we are situated in journeying together, Pope Francis's equanimity during the turbulence surrounding the Synod on the Family and publication of *Amoris Laetitia* invites both courage and hope. Fully committed to journeying together and completely dedicated to sensing the faith, he has taken to heart his own words: "We must continue along this path. The world in which we live, and which we are called to love and serve, even with its contradictions, demands that the Church strengthen cooperation in all areas of her mission. It is precisely this path of *synodality* which God expects of the Church of the third millennium."[21] Indeed, the people of God need courage. But we also need to love and serve one another, acts that imbue lived Christianity with so much hope.

Notes

I. The Authenticity of the Popular

1. Mark Calano, "The Black Nazarene, Quiapo, and the Weak Philippine State," *Kritika Kultura* 25 (2015): 167.

2. Rhochie Avelino Matienzo, "Kierkegaard in Quiapo!: An Existential Look at the Quiapo Black Nazarene Popular Religious Experience," *Scientia* 3, no. 1 (2017): 43–71.

3. Portia Ladrido, "The 'Miracles' of the Black Nazarene," *CNN Philippines Life*, January 11, 2018, https://www.cnnphilippines.com/life/culture/2018/1/9/black-nazarene-devotees.html.

4. Calano, "The Black Nazarene."

5. Calano, "The Black Nazarene," 172.

6. Tim Olaveson, "Collective Effervescence and Communitas: Processual Models of Ritual and Society in Emile Durkheim and Victor Turner," *Dialectical Anthropology* 26 (2001): 89–124.

7. Ira Pedrasa, "Dan Brown Calls Manila 'Gates of Hell' in Novel," *ABS-CBN News*, May 21, 2013, https://news.abs-cbn.com/lifestyle/05/21/13/dan-brown-calls-manila-gates-hell-novel/.

8. Jayeel Cornelio, "Global and Religious: Urban Aspirations and the Governance of Religions in Metro Manila," in *Handbook of Religion and the Asian City: Aspiration and Urbanization in the Twenty-First Century*, ed. Peter van der Veer (Berkeley, CA: University of California Press, 2015), 69–88.

9. Mark Calano, "Ginhawa as Ethic of Panatà: Body Politics and the Devotion to the Black Nazarene," *Budhi* 22, no. 2 (2018): 43–74.

10. Nancy Ammerman, "Introduction: Observing Modern Religious Lives," in *Everyday Religion: Observing Modern Religious Lives*, ed. Nancy Ammerman (Oxford, UK: Oxford University Press, 2007), 3–18.

11. Pope Francis, *With the Smell of the Sheep: The Pope Speaks to Priests, Bishops, and Other Shepherds* (Maryknoll, NY: Orbis, 2017).

12. Lamin Sanneh, *Whose Religion Is Christianity?: The Gospel Beyond the West* (Grand Rapids, MI: Eerdmans, 2001).

13. Sanneh, *Whose Religion*, 22.

14. Paul Joshua Bhakiaraj, "Forms of Asian Indigenous Christianities," in *The Oxford Handbook of Christianity in Asia*, ed. Felix Wilfred (New York: Oxford University Press, 2014), 171–81.

15. Nancy Ammerman, "Lived Religion as an Emerging Field: An Assessment of Its Contours and Frontiers," *Nordic Journal of Religion and Society* 29, no. 2 (2016): 83–99.

16. David Hall, ed., *Lived Religion in America: Toward a History of Practice* (Princeton, NJ: Princeton University Press, 1997).

17. Hall, *Lived Religion in America*, vii–xiii.

18. Ludovic Lado, "Catholicism as a Lived Religion in Africa," *Religion Compass* 14, no. 12 (2020): 1–10.

19. Paul Heelas and Linda Woodhead, *The Spiritual Revolution: Why Religion Is Giving Way to Spirituality* (Oxford, UK: Blackwell, 2015).

20. Robert Fuller, *Spiritual, but Not Religious: Understanding Unchurched America* (New York: Oxford University Press, 2001); Brian J. Zinnbauer et al., "Religion and Spirituality: Unfuzzying the Fuzzy," *Journal for the Scientific Study of Religion* 36, no. 4 (1997): 549–64.

21. Mary Jo Neitz, "Lived Religion: Signposts of Where We Have Been and Where We Can Go from Here," in *Religion, Spirituality, and Everyday Life*, ed. Giuseppe Giordan Jr. and William H. Swatos (London: Springer, 2012), 45–55.

22. Ammerman, "Lived Religion as an Emerging Field."

23. Roman Williams, "Space for God: Lived Religion at Work, Home, and Play," *Sociology of Religion* 71, no. 3 (2013): 257–79.

24. Ammerman, "Introduction: Observing Modern Religious Lives," 6.

25. Linda Woodhead, "Spirituality and Christianity: The Unfolding of a Tangled Relationship," in Giordan and Swatos, eds., *Religion, Spirituality, and Everyday Life*, 3–22.

26. Jayeel Cornelio, *Being Catholic in the Contemporary Philippines: Young People Reinterpreting Religion* (London: Routledge, 2016).

27. Kelly Besecke, "Beyond Literalism: Reflexive Spirituality and Religious Meaning," in Ammerman, ed., *Everyday Religion*, 169–86; Kelly Besecke, *You Can't Put God in a Box: Thoughtful Spirituality in a Rational Age* (New York: Oxford University Press, 2014).

28. Neitz, "Lived Religion," 54.

29. Peter J. Bräunlein, "'We Are 100% Catholic': Philippine Passion Rituals and Some Obstacles in the Study of Non-European Christianity," *Journal of Religion in Europe* 5, no. 3 (2012): 384–413, https://doi.org/doi:10.1163/18748929-00503003.

30. Meredith B. McGuire, *Lived Religion: Faith and Practice in Everyday Life* (Oxford, UK: Oxford University Press, 2008), 185.

31. Lado, *Catholicism*, 6.

32. Bräunlein, "We Are 100%."

33. Robert Cortegiano, "The Use of Sociology in the Study of the *Sensus Fidelium*: An Evaluation of the Contribution of Jerome Baggett," in *Learning from All the Faithful: A Contemporary Theology of the* Sensus Fidei, ed. Bradford Hinze and Peter Phan (Eugene, OR: Pickwick Publications, 2016), 103–21.

34. McGuire, *Lived Religion*, 186.

35. Charles Taylor, *The Ethics of Authenticity* (Cambridge, MA: Harvard University Press, 1991).

36. Linda Woodhead and Paul Heelas, *Religion in Modern Times: An Interpretive Anthology* (Oxford, UK: Blackwell, 2000).

37. Giuseppe Giordan, "Toward a Sociology of Prayer," in Giordan and Swatos, eds., *Religion, Spirituality, and Everyday Life*, 77–88.

38. Giordan, "Toward," 87.

39. Jayeel Cornelio, "Popular Religion and the Turn to Everyday Authenticity: Reflections on the Contemporary Study of Philippine Catholicism," *Philippine Studies: Historical and Ethnographic Viewpoints* 62, no. 3 (2014): 471–500.

40. Jerome P. Baggett, *Sense of the Faithful: How American Catholics Live Their Faith* (Oxford, UK: Oxford University Press, 2009).

41. Nancy Ammerman, "Golden Rule Christianity: Lived Religion in the American Mainstream," in Hall, ed., *Lived Religion in America*, 196–216.

42. Bräunlein, "We Are 100%."

43. Bräunlein, "We Are 100%," 397.

44. Julius Bautista, *The Way of the Cross: Suffering Selfhoods in the Roman Catholic Philippines* (Honolulu, HI: University of Hawai'i Press, 2019).

45. Vicente Rafael, *Contracting Colonialism: Translation and Christian Conversion in Tagalog Society under Early Spanish Rule* (Quezon City, Philippines: Ateneo de Manila University Press, 1988).

46. Cornelio, "Popular Religion."

47. Michael Amaladoss, "Asian Theological Trends," in Wilfred, ed., *The Oxford Handbook of Christianity in Asia*, 106.

48. Amaladoss, "Asian," 112.

49. Peter Phan, "Asian Christian Spirituality," in Wilfred, ed., *The Oxford Handbook of Christianity in Asia*, 520.

50. Susan Dunlap, "Culture-Coded Care: Ecclesial Beliefs, Practices, and Artifacts in Response to Illness," in *Pastoral Bearings: Lived Religion and Pastoral Theology*, ed. Jane Maynard, Leonard Hummel, and Mary Clark Moschella (Lanham, MD: Lexington Books), 75.

51. Dunlap, "Culture-Coded," 75–76.

52. Allan Aubrey Boesak, "The Need for 'A Fighting God': Biko, Black Theology and the Essence of Revolutionary Authenticity," *Black Theology* 18, no. 3 (2020): 201.

53. Boesak, "The Need for a 'Fighting God.'"

54. Adriaan van Klinken, *Kenyan, Christian, Queer: Religion, LGBT Activism, and Arts of Resistance in Africa* (University Park: Pennsylvania State University Press, 2019).

55. Van Klinken, *Kenyan*, 147.

56. Brantley Gasaway, *Progressive Evangelicals and the Pursuit of Social Justice* (Chapel Hill, NC: University of North Carolina Press, 2014).

57. Terence Chong, ed., *Pentecostal Megachurches in Southeast Asia: Negotiating Class, Consumption and the Nation* (Singapore: ISEAS, 2018).

58. Catherine Rivera, "'We Are Overfed': Young Evangelicals, Globalization, and Social Justice," in *The Routledge International Handbook of Religion in Global Society*, ed. Jayeel Cornelio, François Gauthier, Tuomas Martikainen, and Linda Woodhead (London: Routledge), 117–28.

59. For a similar observation, see Jayeel Cornelio, "Young People and Golden Rule Catholicism in the Philippines," in *Christianity in the Modern World: Changes and Controversies*, ed. Giselle Vincett and Elijah Obinna (Farnham, UK: Ashgate, 2014), 11–36.

60. Francis, *With the Smell*.

61. Kim Knibbe, "Is Critique Possible in the Study of Lived Religion? Anthropological and Feminist Reflections," *Journal of Contemporary Religion* 35, no. 2 (2020): 252.

2. The Diversity of Lived Christianity

1. Aurelie Hagstrom, *The Emerging Laity: Vocation, Mission, and Spirituality* (Mahwah, NJ: Paulist Press, 2010).

2. Fabrice Blée, "Can Christians Engage in Non-Christian Practices? Eastern Meditations and Contemplative Prayer," in *Controversies in Contemporary Religions*, ed. Paul Hedges (Santa Barbara, CA: Praeger, 2014), 277–304.

3. Congregation for Divine Worship, *Directory on Popular Piety and the Liturgy: Principles and Guidelines*, December 17, 2001, no. 71, https://www.vatican.va/roman_curia/congregations/ccdds/documents/rc_con_ccdds_doc_20020513_vers-direttorio_en.html.

4. SimonMary Aihiokhai, "A Mosaic of Identities of the *Sensus Fidelium*: The Realities of African Ecclesial Communities in Diaspora," in *Learning from All the Faithful: A Contemporary Theology of the* Sensus Fidei, ed. Bradford Hinze and Peter Phan (Eugene, OR: Pickwick Publications, 2016), 234–35.

5. Nancy Ammerman, "Introduction: Observing Modern Religious Lives," in *Everyday Religion: Observing Modern Religious Lives*, ed. Nancy Ammerman (Oxford, UK: Oxford University Press, 2007), 3–18.

6. Meredith B. McGuire, *Lived Religion: Faith and Practice in Everyday Life* (Oxford, UK: Oxford University Press), 13.

7. Robert Orsi, "Is the Study of Lived Religion Irrelevant to the World We Live In?," *Journal for the Scientific Study of Religion* 42, no. 2 (2003): 172.

8. Michael Mason, "For Youth, Prayer Is Relationship," in *A Sociology of Prayer*, ed. Giuseppe Giordan and Linda Woodhead (Burlington, VT: Ashgate, 2015), 25–48.

9. Daniele Hervieu-Leger, *Religion as a Chain of Memory* (Cambridge, UK: Polity Press, 2000).

10. Vicente Rafael, *Contracting Colonialism: Translation and Christian Conversion in Tagalog Society under Early Spanish Rule* (Quezon City, Philippines: Ateneo de Manila University Press, 1988).

11. Mark Francis, *Local Worship, Global Church: Popular Religion and the Liturgy* (Collegeville, MN: Liturgical Press, 2014), 6.

12. Ormond Rush, *The Eyes of Faith: The Sense of the Faithful and the Church's Reception of Revelation* (Washington, DC: Catholic University of America Press, 2009), 11.

13. Robert Cortegiano, "The Use of Sociology in the Study of the *Sensus Fidelium*: An Evaluation of the Contribution of Jerome Baggett," in Hinze and Phan, eds., *Learning from All the Faithful*, 103–21.

14. Neil Ormerod, "*Sensus Fidei* and Sociology: How Do We Find the Normative in the Empirical?" in *Learning from All the Faithful*, 100.

15. Peter J. Bräunlein, "'We Are 100% Catholic': Philippine Passion Rituals and Some Obstacles in the Study of Non-European Christianity," *Journal of Religion in Europe* 5, no. 3 (2012): 384, https://doi.org/10.1163/18748929-00503003.

16. Jaime Bulatao, *Split-level Christianity* (Manila: Ateneo de Manila University Press, 1966).

17. Jayeel S. Cornelio, "Popular Religion and the Turn to Everyday Authenticity: Reflections on the Contemporary Study of Philippine Catholicism," *Philippine Studies: Historical and Ethnographic Viewpoints* 62, no. 3 (2014): 471–500.

18. McGuire, *Lived Religion*, 213.

19. Francis, *Local Worship*.

20. Eleanor Dionisio, ed., *Becoming a Church of the Poor: Philippine Catholicism after the Second Plenary Council* (Quezon City, Philippines: John J. Carroll Institute on Church and Social Issues, 2011).

21. Amado Picardal, "Environmental Praxis of Basic Ecclesial Communities: An Ecclesiological Perspective," *Hapag: A Journal of Interdisciplinary Theological Research* 8, no. 1 (2012): 57–80.

22. Michele Dillon, *Catholic Identity: Balancing Reason, Faith, and Power* (Cambridge, UK: Cambridge University Press, 1999).

23. Warren Bird, "The World's Largest Churches," Leadership Network, 2013, https://archive.leadnet.org/world.

24. Nicholas Harkness, "Other Christians as Christian Others: Signs of New Christian Populations and the Urban Expansion of Seoul," in *Handbook of Religion and the Asian City: Aspiration and Urbanization in the Twenty-First Century*, ed. Peter van der Veer (Oakland, CA: University of California Press, 2015), 343.

25. Harkness, "Other Christians," 341.

26. Harkness, "Other Christians," 344.

27. Jayeel Cornelio, "Religious Worlding: Christianity and the New Production of Space in the Philippines," in *New Religiosities, Modern Capitalism and Moral Complexities in Southeast Asia*, ed. Juliette Koning and Gwenaël Njoto-Feillard (New York: Palgrave Macmillan, 2017); Elizabeth Olson, "Myth, Miramiento, and the Making of Religious Landscapes," in *Religion and Place: Landscape, Politics and Piety*, ed. Peter Hopkins, Lily Kong, and Elizabeth Olson (Dordrecht, Netherlands: Springer, 2013), 75–94.

28. The location of religion is, of course, not only geographic. As the account above shows, geographic space intersects with embodiment. In other words, understanding the location of the sacred allows us to see its diverse modalities: in place, in the body, in nature, and even in institutions. Our attention for this section is on geography. The next section will probe the embodiment of religion.

29. William Swatos, "Religious Pilgrimage, Pilgrimage Spirituality and Everyday Life," in *Religion, Spirituality and Everyday Practice*, ed. Giuseppe Giordan and William Swatos (Dordrecht, Netherlands: Springer, 2011), 42.

30. Olson, "Myth," 2013.

31. Peter van der Veer, "Introduction," in Van der Veer, ed., *Handbook of Religion and the Asian City*, 11.

32. Jayeel Cornelio, "Global and Religious: Urban Aspirations and the Governance of Religions in Metro Manila," in Van der Veer, ed., *Handbook of Religion and the Asian City*, 69–88; Paul-Francois Tremlett, "Power, Invulnerability, Beauty: Producing and Transforming Male

Bodies in the Lowland Christianised Philippines," *School of Oriental and African Studies' Centre for Gender and Religion Research* (2006), http://oro.open.ac.uk/22473/.

33. Elizabeth Olson, Peter Hopkins, and Lily Kong, "Introduction—Religion and Place: Landscape, Politics, and Piety," in Hopkins et al., *Religion and Place*, 14.

34. Lily Kong, "Christian Evangelizing across National Boundaries: Technology, Cultural Capital and the Intellectualization of Religion," in Hopkins et al., *Religion and Place*, 22.

35. Mellonee Burnim, "Tropes of Continuity and Disjuncture in the Globalization of Gospel Music," in *The Oxford Handbook of Music and World Christianities*, ed. Suzel Ana Reily and Jonathan Dueck (New York: Oxford University Press, 2016), 483.

36. Swatos, "Religious Pilgrimage," 39.

37. Cristián Parker G., "Modern Popular Religion," *International Sociology* 13, no. 2 (1998): 195–212, http://doi.org/10.1177/026858098013002004.

38. Manuel Victor J. Sapitula, "Marian Piety and Modernity: The Perpetual Help Devotion as Popular Religion in the Philippines," *Philippine Studies: Historical & Ethnographic Viewpoints* 62, nos. 3/4 (2014): 399–424.

39. Sapitula, "Marian Piety," 406–7.

40. Robert Orsi, *Between Heaven and Earth: The Religious Worlds People Make and the Scholars Who Study Them* (Princeton, NJ: Princeton University Press, 2005), 74.

41. Maureen Orth, "How the Virgin Mary Became the World's Most Powerful Woman," *National Geographic*, December 2015, https://www.nationalgeographic.com/magazine/article/virgin-mary-worlds-most-powerful-woman.

42. Orth, "How the Virgin Mary."

43. Cornelio, "Popular Religion."

44. G.B. Marcos, "Filipino Religious Fanaticism: Who Is to Blame?," accessed April 25, 2016, http://gbmarcos.blogspot.com/2016/01/filipino-religious-fanaticism-who-is-to.html (blog has been removed).

45. Raymond Boudon, "La rationalité du religieux selon Max Weber," *L'Année sociologique* 51, no. 1 (2001): 9–50.

46. Hervieu-Leger, *Religion*.

47. Parker G., "Modern Popular Religion."

48. Andrew Greeley, *God in Popular Culture* (Chicago: Thomas More Press, 1988), 17.

49. Greeley, *God*, 17.

50. Jayeel Cornelio, "Filipino Catholic Students and Prayer as Conversation with God," in Giordan and Woodhead, eds., *A Sociology of Prayer*, 133–52.

51. Jayeel Cornelio, *Being Catholic in the Contemporary Philippines: Young People Reinterpreting Religion* (London: Routledge, 2016), 68.

3. Lived Christianity as Worship

1. Meredith B. McGuire, *Lived Religion: Faith and Practice in Everyday Life* (Oxford, UK: Oxford University Press, 2008).

2. Congregation for Divine Worship, *Directory on Popular Piety and the Liturgy: Principles and Guidelines*, December 17, 2001, no. 5, https://www.vatican.va/roman_curia/congregations/ccdds/documents/rc_con_ccdds_doc_20020513_vers-direttorio_en.html. Hereafter cited in the text as *Directory*.

3. Mark R. Francis, "Liturgy and Popular Piety in a Historical Perspective," in *Directory on Popular Piety, Principles and Guidelines: A Commentary*, ed. Peter C. Phan (Collegeville, MN: Liturgical Press, 2005), 26.

4. Second Vatican Council, Constitution on the Sacred Liturgy, *Sacrosanctum Concilium*, December 4, 1963, https://www.vatican.va/archive/hist_councils/ii_vatican_council/documents/vat-ii_const_19631204_sacrosanctum-concilium_en.html.

5. James Empereur, "Introduction: Popular Piety and the Liturgy: Principles and Guidelines," in Phan, ed., Directory on Popular Piety, Principles and Guidelines: A Commentary, 1–12.

6. Peter C. Phan, ed., *Directory on Popular Piety, Principles and Guidelines: A Commentary* (Collegeville, MN: Liturgical Press, 2005).

7. Francis, "Liturgy and Popular Piety in a Historical Perspective," 25.

8. Peter E. Fink, "Liturgy and Popular Piety: Piety in the Catholic Magisterium," in Phan, ed., *Directory on Popular Piety*, 54–55.

9. Gustavo Gutiérrez, *A Theology of Liberation: History, Politics and Salvation*, trans. Caridad Inda and John Eagleson (Maryknoll, NY: Orbis Books, 1973), 49.

10. Arthur F. McGovern, *Liberation Theology and Its Critics: Toward an Assessment* (Maryknoll, NY: Orbis Books, 1989), 58.

11. Richard Viladesau, *The Beauty of the Cross* (Oxford, UK: Oxford University Press, 2006), 154–55.

12. Viladesau, *The Beauty of the Cross*, 172.

13. René B. Javellana, ed., *Casaysayan nang pasiong mahal ni Jesucristong Panginoon natin na sucat ipag-alab nang puso nang sinomang babasa* (Quezon City: Ateneo de Manila University Press, 1988). Stanza numbers are indicated in parentheses.

14. Javellana, *Casaysayan nang pasiong mahal*, 11–27.

15. *Pasyon*, st. 352, as quoted in Javellana, ed., *Casaysayan nang pasiong mahal.*

16. *Pasyon*, st. 38, as quoted in Javellana, ed., *Casaysayan nang pasiong mahal.*

17. *Pasyon*, st. 60, as quoted in Javellana, ed., *Casaysayan nang pasiong mahal.*

18. *Pasyon*, st. 253, as quoted in Javellana, ed., *Casaysayan nang pasiong mahal.*

19. Fink, "Liturgy and Popular Piety," 52.

20. Fink, "Liturgy and Popular Piety," 53.

21. Joseph A. Jungmann, *The Mass of the Roman Rite: Its Origins and Development (Missarum Sollemnia)*, 2 vols., trans. Francis A. Brunner (New York: Benziger Brothers, Inc., 1951/1955).

22. Francis, "Liturgy and Popular Piety in a Historical Perspective," 42–43.

23. Fink, "Liturgy and Popular Piety," 53.

24. Gianni Criveller, "Matteo Ricci's Ascent to Beijing," in *Portrait of a Jesuit: Matteo Ricci* (Macau: Macau Ricci Institute, 2004), 39–73.

25. Sangkeun Kim, *Strange Names of God: The Missionary Translation of the Divine Name and the Chinese Responses to Matteo Ricci's "Shangti" in the Late Ming China, 1583–1644* (New York: Peter Lang Publishing, 2004).

26. William Lakos, *Chinese Ancestor Worship: A Practice and Ritual Oriented Approach to Understanding Chinese Culture* (Newcastle upon Tyne, UK: Cambridge Scholars Publishing, 2010), 6.

27. Lakos, *Chinese Ancestor Worship*, 6.

28. Kim, *Strange Names of God*, 187–88.

29. Kim, *Strange Names of God*, 68, 164.

30. Kim, *Strange Names of God*, 272.

31. Jacques Gernet, *China and the Christian Impact: A Conflict of Cultures*, trans. Janet Lloyd (Cambridge: Cambridge University Press, 1985), 5.

32. Gernet, *China and the Christian Impact*, 242.

4. Lived Christianity as Promotion of Liberation

1. Michael R. Candelaria, *Popular Religion and Liberation: The Dilemma of Liberation* (Albany: State University of New York Press, 1990); Orlando O. Espín, *The Faith of the People: Theological Reflections on Popular Catholicism* (Maryknoll, NY: Orbis Books, 1997).

2. See the following early accounts: Arthur F. McGovern, *Liberation Theology and Its Critics: Toward an Assessment* (Maryknoll, NY: Orbis Books, 1989) and Alfred T. Henneley, *Liberation Theology: A Documentary History* (Maryknoll, NY: Orbis Books, 1990). More recent efforts are David Tombs, *Latin American Liberation Theology* (Boston: Brill Academic, 2002) and Gerard Whelan, *A Discerning Church: Pope Francis, Lonergan, and a Theological Method for the Future* (Mahwah, NJ: Paulist Press, 2019).

3. Candelaria, *Popular Religion and Liberation*, xiii.

4. McGovern, *Liberation Theology and Its Critics*, 7–8.

5. Hilari Raguer, "An Initial Profile of the Assembly," in *History of Vatican II*, vol. 2, ed. Giuseppe Alberigo, English ed. Joseph A. Komonchak (Maryknoll, NY: Orbis and Leuven, Belgium: Peeters, 1997), 194–221.

6. Raguer, "An Initial Profile," 204.

7. Raguer, "An Initial Profile," 207.

8. Raguer, "An Initial Profile," 202.

9. Giuseppe Alberigo, "Transition to a New Age," in *History of Vatican II*, vol. 5, ed. Giuseppe Alberigo, English ed. Joseph A. Komonchak (Maryknoll, NY: Orbis and Leuven, Belgium: Peeters, 2006), 608.

10. Whelan, *A Discerning Church*, 91.

11. Ivan Petrella, *The Future of Liberation Theology: An Argument and Manifesto* (Hampshire, UK: Ashgate, 2003), 106.

12. Whelan, *A Discerning Church*, 91–92.

13. Cited in Candelaria, *Popular Religion and Liberation*, 40.

14. McGovern, *Liberation Theology and Its Critics*, 235–39.

15. Petrella, *The Future of Liberation Theology*, 146.

16. McGovern, *Liberation Theology and Its Critics*, 7.

17. Whelan, *A Discerning Church*, 91.

18. Whelan, *A Discerning Church*, 177.

19. Tombs, *Latin American Liberation Theology*, 273.

20. Tombs, *Latin American Liberation Theology*, 273.

21. Aloysius Pieris, *An Asian Theology of Liberation* (Maryknoll, NY: Orbis Books), 1988.

22. See the following: David Batstone et al., eds., *Liberation Theologies, Postmodernity, and the Americas* (London: Routledge, 1997); Miguel de la Torre, ed., *Introducing Liberative Theologies* (Maryknoll, NY: Orbis Books, 2015); and Goetz Franz Ottmann, *Lost for Words? Brazilian Liberationism in the 1990s* (Pittsburgh, PA: University of Pittsburgh Press, 2002).

23. Candelaria, *Popular Religion and Liberation*, 103.

24. Candelaria, *Popular Religion and Liberation*, 106.

25. Walter Kasper, *Pope Francis' Revolution of Tenderness and Love: Theological and Pastoral Perspectives* (Mahwah, NJ: Paulist Press, 2015), 19.

26. Candelaria, *Popular Religion and Liberation*, 7.

27. Kasper, *Pope Francis' Revolution*, 20.

28. Whelan, *A Discerning Church*, 98.

29. Candelaria, *Popular Religion and Liberation*, 16–17.

30. Candelaria, *Popular Religion and Liberation*, 50.

31. Candelaria, *Popular Religion and Liberation*, 51.

32. José Miguez Bonino, "Popular Piety in Latin America," *Concilium* 96 (1974): 154.

33. Harvey Cox, "Seven Samurai and How They Looked Again: Theology, Social Analysis, and *Religión Popular* in Latin America," in *The Future of Liberation Theology: Essays in Honor of Gustavo Gutiérrez*, ed. Marc H. Ellis and Otto Maduro (Maryknoll, NY: Orbis Books, 1989), 234.

34. Segundo Galilea, "Popular Piety in Latin America," *Concilium* 96 (1974): 41.

35. José Miguez Bonino, "La Piedad Popular in America Latina," *Cristianismo y Sociedad* 47 (1976): 31–38.

36. Cox, "Seven Samurai," 234.

37. Cox, "Seven Samurai," 235.

38. Cox, "Seven Samurai," 234.

39. Cox, "Seven Samurai," 235.

40. Juan Luis Segundo, *Liberation of Theology*, trans. John Drury (Maryknoll, NY: Orbis Books, 1976), 187.

41. Segundo, *Liberation of Theology*, 187.

42. Segundo Galilea, *The Challenge of Popular Religiosity* (Quezon City, Philippines: Claretian Publications, 1988). This Philippine edition was published because of similarities between Philippine and Latin American contexts.

43. Segundo Galilea, "La fe como principio critico de promoción de la religiosidad popular," in *Fe cristiana y cambio social en América latina*, ed. Instituto Fe y Secularidad (Salamanca: Ediciones Sígueme, 1973), 157.

44. Segundo Galilea, "The Theology of Liberation and the Place of 'Folk Religion,'" *Concilium* 136, no. 6 (1980); See also Appendix A of Galilea, *The Challenge of Popular Religiosity*, 94.

45. Juan Carlos Scannone, "Theology, Popular Culture, and Discernment," in *Frontiers of Theology in Latin America*, ed. Rosino Gibellini (Maryknoll, NY: Orbis Books, 1979), 226.

46. Scannone, "Theology," 227.

47. Candelaria, *Popular Religion and Liberation*, 41.

48. Juan Carlos Scannone, "Pope Francis and the Theology of the People," *Theological Studies* 77, no. 1 (March 2016): 124.

49. Scannone, *Teología de liberación y praxis popular: aportes críticos para una teología de la liberación* (Salamanca: Ediciones Sígueme, 1976), 246, quoted in Candelaria, *Popular Religion and Liberation*, 51.

50. Kasper, *Pope Francis' Revolution*, 19.

51. Quoted in Cox, "Seven Samurai," 236.

52. Candelaria, *Popular Religion and Liberation*, 66.

53. Scannone, *Teología*, 237, quoted in Candelaria, *Popular Religion and Liberation*, 66.

54. Scannone, "Pope Francis and the Theology of the People," 120.

55. Candelaria, *Popular Religion and Liberation*, 56–57.

56. Scannone, "Pope Francis and the Theology of the People," 120.

57. Scannone, "Pope Francis and the Theology of the People," 120.
58. Scannone, "Pope Francis and the Theology of the People," 120.
59. Scannone, "Pope Francis and the Theology of the People," 122.
60. Candelaria, *Popular Religion and Liberation*, 65.
61. Segundo, *Liberation of Theology*, 185.
62. Segundo, *Liberation of Theology*, 190.
63. Segundo, *Liberation of Theology*, 185.
64. Candelaria, *Popular Religion and Liberation*, 41–42.
65. Segundo, *Liberation of Theology*, 188.
66. Segundo, *Liberation of Theology*, 226.
67. Segundo, *Liberation of Theology*, 190.
68. Segundo, *Liberation of Theology*, 190.
69. Segundo, *Liberation of Theology*, 231.
70. Meredith B. McGuire, *Lived Religion: Faith and Practice in Everyday Life* (Oxford, UK: Oxford University Press, 2008), 5.
71. McGuire, *Lived Religion*, 12.
72. Reynaldo Clemeña Ileto, *Pasyon and Revolution: Popular Movements in the Philippines, 1840–1910* (Quezon City, Philippines: Ateneo de Manila University Press), 15.
73. Ileto, *Pasyon and Revolution*, 17–18.
74. Caroline Walker Bynum, *Holy Feast and Holy Fast: The Religious Significance of Food to Medieval Women* (Berkeley: University of California Press, 1987), 296.
75. Bynum, *Holy Feast and Holy Fast*, 296.
76. McGuire, *Lived Religion*, 12.
77. McGuire, *Lived Religion*, 15–16.
78. Candelaria, *Popular Religion and Liberation*, 66.
79. Scannone, *Teología*, 237, quoted in Candelaria, *Popular Religion and Liberation*, 66.
80. This theological view of lived Christianity resonates with the sociological approach we spelled out in part 1.
81. Espín, *The Faith of the People*, 73–74.
82. Jeanette Rodriguez, *Our Lady of Guadalupe: Faith and Empowerment among Mexican-American Women* (Austin, TX: University of Texas Press, 1994), 1–15.
83. Espín, *The Faith of the People*, 75.
84. A. M. Garibay, "Guadalupe, Our Lady," in *New Catholic Encyclopedia*, 2nd ed., ed. Bernard Marthaler et al. (Washington, DC: Catholic University of America Press, 2003), 547–48.

85. Espín, *The Faith of the People*, 77.
86. Espín, *The Faith of the People*, 8.
87. Espín, *The Faith of the People*, 9.
88. Espín, *The Faith of the People*, 9.

5. Lived Christianity and Christian Tradition

1. Yves M-J Congar, *Tradition and Traditions: A Historical and Theological Essay* (London: Burns & Oates, 1966); Yves M-J Congar, *The Meaning of Tradition* (San Francisco: Ignatius Press, 2004).

2. *Catechism of the Catholic Church* (Manila: ECCCE, Word and Life Publications, 1994), §83.

3. Gerald O'Collins, *Tradition: Understanding Christian Tradition* (Oxford, UK: Oxford University Press, 2018).

4. Meredith McGuire, *Lived Religion: Faith and Practice in Everyday Life* (Oxford, UK: Oxford University Press, 2006), 22.

5. Found in P. C. Rodger and L. Vischer, eds., "The Report of the Theological Commission on 'Tradition and Traditions,'" in *The Fourth World Conference on Faith and Order, Montreal 1963* (London: SCM Press, 1966), 3–63; henceforth *Montreal Report 1963*.

6. O'Collins, *Tradition*, 18.

7. O'Collins, *Tradition*, 11–12 on *Dei Verbum* 2 (see n. 13 below) and *Montreal Report 1963*, 51.

8. *Montreal Report 1963*, 54; italics from O'Collins, *Tradition*, 13.

9. O'Collins, *Tradition*, 12.

10. *Montreal Report 1963*, 51.

11. Harold C. Skillrud, J. Francis Stafford, and Daniel F. Martensen, eds., *Scripture and Tradition: Lutherans and Catholics in Dialogue IX* (Minneapolis, MN: Augsburg Fortress Press, 1995).

12. O'Collins, *Tradition*, 12.

13. Vatican Council II, *Dei Verbum* (Dogmatic Constitution on Divine Revelation), November 18, 1965, https://www.vatican.va/archive/hist_councils/ii_vatican_council/documents/vat-ii_const_19651118_dei-verbum_en.html.

14. *Montreal Report 1963*, 52, quoted in O'Collins, *Tradition*, 13.

15. McGuire, *Lived Religion: Faith and Practice in Everyday Life* (Oxford, UK: Oxford University Press, 2006), 12.

16. O'Collins, *Tradition*, 68.

17. O'Collins, *Tradition*, 65–66.

18. Vatican Council II, *Unitatis Redintegratio*, no. 17, quoted in O'Collins, *Tradition*, 15.

19. Robert J. Schreiter, *Constructing Local Theologies* (Maryknoll, NY: Orbis Books, 1985), 21.

20. Orlando O. Espín, *Idol & Grace: On Traditioning and Subversive Hope* (Maryknoll, NY: Orbis Books, 2014), 114.

21. Espín, *Idol & Grace*, 35.

22. Espín, *Idol & Grace*, 36.

23. Espín, *Idol & Grace*, 37.

24. Congar, *The Meaning of Tradition*, 51.

25. Congar, *The Meaning of Tradition*, 51.

26. Congar, *The Meaning of Tradition*, 53.

27. Congar, *The Meaning of Tradition*, 57.

28. Congar, *The Meaning of Tradition*, 53.

29. Congar, *The Meaning of Tradition*, 55.

30. Congar, *The Meaning of Tradition*, 54.

31. Congar, *Tradition and Traditions*, 321.

32. Congar, *Tradition and Traditions*, 327.

33. O'Collins, *Tradition*, 71.

34. Congar, *Tradition and Traditions*, 327.

35. Congar, *Tradition and Traditions*, 328.

36. Philip Pettit, "Agency-Freedom and Option-Freedom," *Journal of Theoretical Politics* 15, no. 4 (2003): 387–403.

37. Congar, *The Meaning of Tradition*, 54.

38. Raimon Panikkar, "On Christian Identity, Who Is a Christian?" in *Many Mansions?: Multiple Religious Belonging and Christian Identity*, ed. Catherine Cornille (Maryknoll, NY: Orbis Books, 2002), 104.

39. Claude Geffre, "Double Belonging and the Originality of Christianity as a Religion," in Cornille, ed., *Many Mansions?*, 98.

40. Ajit K. Maan, *Internarrative Identity* (Lanham, MD: University Press of America, 1999), 65.

41. Terrence W. Tilley, *Inventing Catholic Tradition* (Maryknoll, NY: Orbis Books, 2000), 13–44.

42. Jose Mario C. Francisco, "Christian without Borders: Impossible? Imperative? A View from Asia," *Christian Identity I* / Christliche Identitaet *I Forum Mission* 2 (2006): 12–28.

43. O'Collins, *Tradition*, 59.

44. Francisco Blancas de San Jose, *Vocabulario de la lengua tagala* (1609?); Juan Jose Noceda and Pedro Sanlucar, *Vocabulario de la lengua tagala (1764)*, ed. Virgilio Almario (Quezon City, Philippines: Komisyon ng Wikang Filipino, 2013).

45. Kathryn Tanner, *Theories of Culture: A New Agenda for Theology* (Minneapolis, MN: Fortress Press, 1997), 150.

46. Jan N. Pieterse, "Globalization as Hybridization," in *Global Modernities*, ed. M. Featherstone, S. Lash, and R. Robertson (London: Sage Publications, 1995), 47–68; Robert J. Schreiter, *The New Catholicity: Theology between the Global and the Local* (Maryknoll, NY: Orbis Books, 1997), 74–78.

47. Michael L. Budde, *The Borders of Baptism: Identities, Allegiances, and the Church* (Eugene, OR: Cascade Books, 2011), 23.

48. Catherine Cornille, "Globalization and the Challenges of Hybrid Religious Identities" (paper presented at the conference on Religious Identities in a Globalized World, University of Münster, June 9–12, 2016).

49. Albertus Bagus Laksana, "Multiple Religious Belonging or Complex Identity? An Asian Way of Being Religious," in *The Oxford Handbook of Christianity in Asia*, ed. Felix Wilfred (New York: Oxford University Press, 2014), 493–500.

50. McGuire, *Lived Religion*, 22–25.

51. Ari Dy, *Chinese Buddhism in Catholic Philippines: Syncretism as Identity* (Mandaluyong City, Philippines: Anvil, 2016), 209–34.

52. Hans-Georg Gadamer, *Truth and Method* (New York: Crossroad, 1982); Jürgen Habermas, "A Review of Gadamer's *Truth and Method*," in *Understanding and Social Inquiry*, ed. Fred R. Dallmayer and Thomas A. McCarthy (Notre Dame: University of Notre Dame Press, 1977), 335–63; Paul Ricoeur, "Hermeneutics and the Critique of Ideology," in *Hermeneutics and the Human Sciences: Essays on Language, Action and Interpretation*, ed. John B. Thompson (Cambridge, UK: Cambridge University Press, 1981), 63–100.

53. Ricoeur, "Hermeneutics and the Critique of Ideology," in Thompson, ed., *Hermeneutics and the Human Sciences*, 63.

54. Gadamer, *Truth and Method*, 321.
55. Gadamer, *Truth and Method*, 324.
56. O'Collins, *Tradition*, 47.
57. Dale T. Irvin, *Christian Histories, Christian Traditioning: Rendering Accounts* (Maryknoll, NY: Orbis Books, 1998), xi.
58. Tilley, *Inventing Catholic Tradition*, 43.
59. Congar, *The Meaning of Tradition*, 55.
60. Gadamer, *Truth and Method*, 324.
61. Gadamer, *Truth and Method*, 240.
62. Ricoeur, "Hermeneutics and the Critique of Ideology," 95.
63. Habermas, "A Review of Gadamer's *Truth and Method*," 357.
64. Habermas, "A Review of Gadamer's *Truth and Method*," 360.
65. Habermas, "A Review of Gadamer's *Truth and Method*," 360.
66. Habermas, "A Review of Gadamer's *Truth and Method*," 361. (Italics in the original.)
67. Jürgen Habermas, *The Theory of Communicative Action*, vols. 1 and 2, trans. Thomas McCarthy (Boston: Beacon Press, 1984 and 1985).
68. Ricoeur, "Hermeneutics and the Critique of Ideology," 64.
69. Paul Ricoeur, *Interpretation Theory: Discourse and the Surplus of Meaning* (Fort Worth: Texas Christian University Press, 1976).
70. Ricoeur, "Hermeneutics and the Critique of Ideology," 95.
71. Ricoeur, "Hermeneutics and the Critique of Ideology," 96.
72. Ricoeur, "Hermeneutics and the Critique of Ideology," 97.
73. Ricoeur, "Hermeneutics and the Critique of Ideology," 99.
74. "International Congress on Mission Consensus Paper Workshop II, no. 6," in *For All the Peoples of Asia: Federation of Asian Bishops' Conferences Documents from 1970 to 1991*, vol. 1, ed. Gaudencio B. Rosales and C. G. Arevalo (Quezon City: Claretian Publications, 1992), 138.
75. O'Collins, *Tradition*, 136.
76. Vatican Council II, *Gaudium et Spes* (The Pastoral Constitution on the Church in the Modern World), December 7, 1965, https://www.vatican.va/archive/hist_councils/ii_vatican_council/documents/vat-ii_const_19651207_gaudium-et-spes_en.html.
77. Congar, *Tradition and Traditions*, 425–58; Congar, *The Meaning of Tradition*, 129–55.
78. Congar, *The Meaning of Tradition*, 151.
79. Congar, *The Meaning of Tradition*, 126.

80. Congar, *The Meaning of Tradition*, 122.

81. Congar, *The Meaning of Tradition*, 115.

82. John E. Thiel, *Senses of Tradition: Continuity and Development in Catholic Faith* (Oxford, UK: Oxford University Press, 2000).

83. See W.S. Sykes, *The Identity of Christianity: Theologians and the Essence of Christianity from Schleiermacher to Barth* (Minneapolis, MN: Fortress Press, 1984).

84. Ricoeur, *Interpretation Theory*, 29–30.

85. Ricoeur, *Interpretation Theory*, 31–32.

86. Ricoeur, *Interpretation Theory*, 87–88.

87. See Sandra Schneiders, *The Revelatory Text: Interpreting the New Testament as Scripture* (Minneapolis, MN: Liturgical Press, 1999), which applies this phrase to Scripture within the framework of Ricoeur's hermeneutics.

88. Pope Francis, apostolic exhortation *Evangelii Gaudium* (The Joy of the Gospel), November 24, 2013, https://www.vatican.va/content/francesco/en/apost_exhortations/documents/papa-francesco_esortazione-ap_20131124_evangelii-gaudium.html.

6. A Theological Exploration of Marian Practice

1. Julius J. Bautista, *Figuring Catholicism: An Ethnohistory of the Santo Niño de Cebu* (Quezon City, Philippines: Ateneo de Manila University Press, 2010).

2. Bautista, *Figuring Catholicism*, 1.

3. For instance, lists of apparitions are found in Abraham Varghese, *God-Sent: A History of the Accredited Apparitions of Mary* (New York: Crossroad, 2000) and on the University of Dayton (Ohio) website, with 389 Marian apparitions from 1900 to 2011 and their status: https://udayton.edu/imri/mary/a/apparitions-statistics-modern.php.

4. Aside from recent Protestant reflections on devotional practice in general and on Mary's place within Christology in particular, some Protestants have been known to engage in pilgrimages or the Stations of the Cross devotion.

5. See some recent examples: Stephen Benko, *The Virgin Goddess: Studies in the Pagan and Christian Roots of Mariology* (Leiden,

Netherlands: E.J. Brill, 1993); Sarah Jane Boss, *Empress and Handmaid: On Nature and Gender in the Cult of the Virgin Mary* (London: Cassell, 2000); and Francis X. Clooney, *Divine Mother, Blessed Mother: Hindu Goddesses and the Virgin Mary* (Oxford, UK: Oxford University Press, 2005).

6. See Donna Spivey Ellington, *From Sacred Body to Angelic Soul: Understanding Mary in Late Medieval and Early Modern Europe* (Washington, DC: Catholic University Press, 2001), 248–59.

7. See, e.g., D.A. Brading, *Mexican Phoenix: Our Lady of Guadalupe: Image and Tradition across Five Centuries* (Cambridge, UK: Cambridge University Press, 2001); William A. Christian Jr., *Visionaries: The Spanish Republic and the Reign of Christ* (Berkeley: University of California Press, 1996); and Mart Bax, *Medjugorje: Religion, Politics, and Violence in Rural Bosnia* (Amsterdam: VU Uitgeverij, 1995).

8. Dierdre de la Cruz, *Mother Figured: Marian Apparitions and the Making of a Filipino Universal* (Chicago: University of Chicago Press, 2015), 8.

9. De la Cruz, *Mother Figured*, 7.

10. Ellington, *From Sacred Body*, 246.

11. Ellington, *From Sacred Body*, 186–87.

12. Ellington, *From Sacred Body*, 181.

13. Ellington, *From Sacred Body*, 247.

14. Ellington, *From Sacred Body*, 26–27.

15. Ellington, *From Sacred Body*, 45.

16. Ellington, *From Sacred Body*, 30.

17. De la Cruz, *Mother Figured*, 7.

18. De la Cruz, *Mother Figured*, 7.

19. John N. Schumacher, *Readings in Philippine Church History* (Quezon City: Loyola School of Theology, 1979), 74–75.

20. De la Cruz, *Mother Figured*, 6.

21. Brading, *Mexican Phoenix*, 11.

22. Brading, *Mexican Phoenix*, 77. Also see Luis Becerra Tanco, "The Felicity of Mexico in the Wonderful Apparition of the Virgin Mary, Our Lady of Guadalupe," in *The Dark Virgin: The Book of Our Lady of Guadalupe—A Documentary Anthology*, ed. Donald Demarest and Coley Taylor (New York: Coley Taylor, 1956), 112.

23. Brading, *Mexican Phoenix*, 103.

24. Victor Turner and Edith Turner, *Image and Pilgrimage in Christian Culture* (New York: Columbia University Press, 1978), 208.

25. M. Aladel, *The Miraculous Medal, Its Origin, History, Circulation, Results*, trans. P.S. from French edition (Philadelphia: H. L. Kilner & Co., 1880), 55, quoted in De la Cruz, *Mother Figured*, 8.

26. De la Cruz, *Mother Figured*, 9.

27. CDF, "The Message of Fatima," June 26, 2000, https://www.vatican.va/roman_curia/congregations/cfaith/documents/rc_con_cfaith_doc_20000626_message-fatima_en.html.

28. CDF, "Introduction," in "The Message of Fatima." Since the document contains no page or paragraph numbers, the title of the section containing the quotation is given.

29. Bax, *Medjugorje*.

30. Bax, *Medjugorje*, xvi and 114.

31. Christian, *Visionaries*, 7.

32. Christian, *Visionaries*, xx.

33. Quoted in Christian, *Visionaries*, 29.

34. Christian, *Visionaries*, 6–9.

35. Christian, *Visionaries*, 392–96.

36. Christian, *Visionaries*, 1.

37. Christian, *Visionaries*, 392–402.

38. Christian, *Visionaries*, 392.

39. Christian, *Visionaries*, 394.

40. Christian, *Visionaries*, 402.

41. Christian, *Visionaries*, 8.

42. Orlando O. Espín, *The Faith of the People: Theological Reflection on Popular Catholicism* (Maryknoll, NY: Orbis Books, 1997), 9.

43. Espín, *The Faith of the People*, 9.

44. CDF, "Theological Commentary," in "The Message of Fatima."

45. Quoted in "The Message of Fatima."

46. CDF, "Theological Commentary," in "The Message of Fatima."

47. Espín, *The Faith of the People*, 75.

48. Jose Mario C. Francisco, "Speaking in Many Tongues: Translation and Transcendence in Early Filipino Christianity," *Budhi* 13, nos. 1–3 (2009): 605–15.

49. Orlando O. Espín, *Idol and Grace: On Traditioning and Subversive Hope* (Maryknoll, NY: Orbis Books, 2014), 73.

50. Espín, *Idol and Grace*, 74.

51. Espín, *The Faith of the People*, 76.

52. Espín, *The Faith of the People*, 76.

53. Espín, *The Faith of the People*, 73.

54. Espín, *The Faith of the People*, 76.

55. Espín, *The Faith of the People*, 75.

56. See Brading, *Mexican Phoenix*, 132–39, 317–22, and 338–41.

57. Paul Ricoeur, *Interpretation Theory: Discourse and the Surplus of Meaning* (Fort Worth, TX: Texas Christian University Press, 1976), 41.

58. Ricoeur, *Interpretation Theory*, 42.

59. Brading, *Mexican Phoenix*, 361.

60. Brading, *Mexican Phoenix*, 363.

61. Brading, *Mexican Phoenix*, 363.

62. Brading, *Mexican Phoenix*, 363.

63. Brading, *Mexican Phoenix*, 368.

64. Brading, *Mexican Phoenix*, 365.

65. Hans-Georg Gadamer, *Truth and Method* (New York: Crossroad, 1982), 257.

66. Carmen Nanko-Fernandez, "From *Parajo* to Paraclete: Retrieving the Spirit of God in the Company of Mary," in *Building Bridges, Doing Justice: Constructing a Latino/a Ecumenical Theology*, ed. Orlando O. Espín (Maryknoll, NY: Orbis Books, 2009), 19.

67. Miguel Diaz, *On Being Human: U.S. Hispanic and Rahnerian Perspectives* (Maryknoll, NY: Orbis Books, 2001), 125; quoted in Nanko-Fernandez, "From *Parajo* to Paraclete," 19.

68. Espín, *The Faith of the People*, 76.

69. De la Cruz, *Mother Figured*, 209–12.

70. Antonio F. B. de Castro, "La Virgen del Pilar: Defamiliarizing Mary and the Challenge of Interreligious Dialogue," *Landas* 19, no. 1 (2005): 57–91.

71. John Christian U. Young, "Dialogue at the Margins, Popular Religiosity in Mindanao as an Approach to Inter-religious Dialogue" (STD diss., Pontifical Gregorian University, 2015).

72. Espín, *The Faith of the People*, 73.

7. Lived Christianity as *Sensus Fidei*

1. Ormond Rush, *The Eyes of Faith: The Sense of the Faithful and the Church's Reception of Revelation* (Washington, DC: Catholic University of America Press, 2009), 9.

2. International Theological Commission, Sensus Fidei *in the Life of the Church*, 2014, https://www.vatican.va/roman_curia/congregations/cfaith/cti_documents/rc_cti_20140610_sensus-fidei_en.html. (Citations hereafter in the text).

3. Rush, *The Eyes of Faith*, 9.

4. Meredith B. McGuire, *Lived Religion: Faith and Practice in Everyday Life* (Oxford, UK: Oxford University Press, 2008), 13–16.

5. Claire Watkins et al., "Practical Ecclesiology: What Counts as Theology in Studying the Church?" in *Perspectives on Ecclesiology and Ethnography*, ed. Peter Ward (Grand Rapids, MI: Eerdmans, 2012), 168.

6. Rush, *The Eyes of Faith*, 241.

7. Rush, *The Eyes of Faith*, 70.

8. See Anthony Ekpo, "The *Sensus Fidelium* and the Threefold Office of Christ: A Reinterpretation of *Lumen Gentium* No. 12," *Theological Studies* 76, no. 2 (2016): 330–46. Ekpo argues that *Lumen Gentium* 12 discusses the *sensus fidelium* in relation to the teaching office only and not to the priestly and kingly offices of Christ.

9. Gerard Mannion, "*Sensus Fidelium* and the International Theological Commission—Has Anything Changed between 2012 and 2014?" in *Learning from All the Faithful: A Contemporary Theology of the* Sensus Fidei, ed. Bradford E. Hinze and Peter C. Phan (Eugene, OR: Pickwick Publications, 2016), 77.

10. Rush, *The Eyes of Faith*, 280.

11. Rush, *The Eyes of Faith*, 280–81.

12. See Richard R. Gaillardetz, *By What Authority? Foundations for Understanding Authority in the Church* (Collegeville, MN: Liturgical Press, 2018).

13. Mannion, "*Sensus Fidelium*," 83.

14. Jeannine Hill Fletcher, "Supremacy in the Sense of the Faithful: Theological Anthropology and the 'Various Ranks' (*Lumen Gentium* 13)," in Hinze and Phan, eds., *Learning from All the Faithful*, 53.

15. Aside from individual works, the following anthologies are useful: Daniel J. Finucane, *Sensus Fidelium: The Use of a Concept in the Post–Vatican II Era* (London: International Scholars, 1996); and Bradford E. Hinze and Peter C. Phan, eds., *Learning from All the Faithful: A Contemporary Theology of the* Sensus Fidei (Eugene, OR: Pickwick Publications, 2016).

16. See Christian Scharen, *Field Work in Theology* (Grand Rapids, MI: Baker Academic, 2015); and the multiauthor anthology edited by Christian Scharen, *Explorations in Ecclesiology and Ethnography* (Grand Rapids, MI: Eerdmans, 2012).

17. See Neil Ormerod, "*Sensus Fidei* and Sociology: How Do We Find the Normative in the Empirical?" in Hinze and Phan, eds., Learning from All the Faithful, 89–102.

18. Robert S. Fiddes, "Ecclesiology and Ethnography: Two Disciplines, Two Worlds," in *Perspectives on Ecclesiology and Ethnography*, ed. Peter Ward (Grand Rapids, MI: Eerdmans, 2012), 14.

19. Robert Orsi, *Between Heaven and Hell: The Religious Worlds People Make and the Scholars Who Study Them* (Princeton, NJ: Princeton University Press, 2005), 147.

20. Fiddes, "Ecclesiology and Ethnography," 17–24.

21. Bradford Hinze, *Prophetic Obedience: Ecclesiology for a Dialogical Church* (Maryknoll, NY: Orbis Books, 2016); Jerome P. Baggett, *Sense of the Faithful: How American Catholics Live Their Faith* (New York: Oxford University Press, 2009).

22. Hinze, *Prophetic Obedience*, 9–36.

23. Hinze, *Prophetic Obedience*, 22.

24. Hinze, *Prophetic Obedience*, 36.

25. Hinze, *Prophetic Obedience*, 22.

26. Hinze, *Prophetic Obedience*, 52–55.

27. Hinze, *Prophetic Obedience*, 55.

28. CDF, "Letter to the Bishops of the Catholic Church on Some Aspects of the Church Understood as Communion," May 28, 1992, https://www.vatican.va/roman_curia/congregations/cfaith/documents/rc_con_cfaith_doc_28051992_communionis-notio_en.html.

29. See Hinze, *Prophetic Obedience*, 37–72; and Gerard Whelan, *A Discerning Church: Pope Francis, Lonergan and a Theological Method for the Future* (Mahwah, NJ: Paulist Press, 2019), 71–89.

30. Baggett, *Sense of the Faithful*, appendices A and B, 241–46.

31. Baggett, *Sense of the Faithful*, 14, quoting Will Herberg,

Protestant, Catholic, Jew: An Essay in American Religious Society (Garden City, NJ: Doubleday, 1960), 133.

32. Baggett, *Sense of the Faithful*, 13.

33. Baggett, *Sense of the Faithful*, 66.

34. See illustrations in the quotes from Sarah Henslin and Dale Perrow in Baggett, *Sense of the Faithful*, 69 and 106 respectively.

35. Baggett, *Sense of the Faithful*, 21. The phrase is borrowed from Marie Therese Winter et al., *Defecting in Place: Women Claiming Responsibility for Their Own Spiritual Lives* (New York: Crossroad, 1994), 114–15.

36. Baggett, *Sense of the Faithful*, 21.

37. Baggett, *Sense of the Faithful*, 87–88.

38. Baggett, *Sense of the Faithful*, 21.

39. Baggett, *Sense of the Faithful*, 156–57.

40. Baggett, *Sense of the Faithful*, 201.

41. Baggett, *Sense of the Faithful*, 94–95.

42. Baggett, *Sense of the Faithful*, 210.

43. Hinze, *Prophetic Obedience*, 72.

44. Robert Cortegiano, "The Use of Sociology in the Study of the *Sensus Fidelium*: An Evaluation of the Contribution of Jerome Baggett," in Hinze and Phan, eds., *Learning from All the Faithful*, 115.

45. Hinze, *Prophetic Obedience*, 51.

46. Walter Kasper, *The Catholic Church: Nature, Reality and Mission* (London: Bloomsbury T&T Clark, 2015), 14.

47. See the conference proceedings in Antonio Spadaro and Carlos Mariá Galli, eds., *La Riforma e le Riforme nella Chiesa* (Brescia, Italy: Queriniana, 2016).

48. James Nieman and Roger Haight, "On the Dynamic Relation between Ecclesiology and Congregational Studies," in *Explorations in Ecclesiology and Ethnography*, ed. Christian Scharen (Grand Rapids, MI: Eerdmans, 2012), 11.

49. Nieman and Haight, "On the Dynamic," 12–13.

50. See recent studies on Galtung's theory in Kees van der Veer et al., *Multidimensional Social Science: An Inclusive Approach to Social Position and Inequality* (Rotterdam, Netherlands: Rozenberg Publishers, 2009); For instance, see Samir Amin, *Unequal Development* (Sussex, UK: Harvester Press, 1976); and Fernando Henrique Cardoso and Enzo Faletto, *Dependency and Development in Latin America* (Berkeley: University of California Press, 1979).

51. Pasquale Ferrara, "The Concept of Peripheries in Pope Francis' Discourse: A Religious Challenge to Globalization?," *Religions* 6 (2016): 42, https://doi.org/10.3390/rel6010042.

52. Pope Francis, as quoted in Ferrera, "The Concept of Peripheries," 50.

53. Andrea Tornielli, "Tentazione sudamericana per il primo Papa extraeuropeo," *La Stampa*, March 2, 2013, https://www.lastampa.it/cronaca/2013/03/02/news/tentazione-sudamericana-1.36108674/.

54. Antonio Spadaro, "Wake Up the World. Conversations with Pope Francis about Religious Life," *La Civiltá Cattolica* 1 (2014): 3–17, at 3–4. English translation of original Italian text by Fr. Donald Maldari, SJ.

55. Michel de Certeau, *The Practice of Everyday Life*, trans. David Rendall (Berkeley: University of California Press, 1984).

56. Kasper, *The Catholic Church*, 3.

57. Kasper, *The Catholic Church*, 3.

58. Kasper, *The Catholic Church*, 333.

8. Theology and Sociology

1. Pope Francis, *With the Smell of the Sheep: The Pope Speaks to Priests, Bishops, and Other Shepherds* (Maryknoll, NY: Orbis Books, 2017).

2. Jayeel Cornelio, "Popular Religion and the Turn to Everyday Authenticity: Reflections on the Contemporary Study of Philippine Catholicism," *Philippine Studies: Historical and Ethnographic Viewpoints* 62, no. 3 (2014).

3. Rowena Robinson, "'Smell Your Sheep, Shepherd': What Does It Mean to Be Catholic for the Dalit?," *Religions* 10, no. 659 (2019): 8.

4. Pope Francis, *With the Smell of the Sheep*.

5. Emilce Cuda, "Pope Francis: It Is the Politics!," *The Politics and Religion Journal—Serbian Edition* 11, no. 1 (2017): 110.

6. Kieran Flanagan, "The Return of Theology: Sociology's Distant Relative," in *The Blackwell Companion to Sociology of Religion*, ed. Richard Fenn (Malden, MA: Blackwell, 2001), 432–44.

7. John Brewer, "Sociology and Theology Reconsidered:

Religious Sociology and the Sociology of Religion in Britain," *History of the Human Sciences* 20, no. 2 (2007): 7–28.

8. Daniel Franklin Pilario, "Interdisciplinary Perspectives and Approaches in Theologizing in Asia," *International Journal of Indonesian Philosophy & Theology* 1, no. 1 (2020): 29–42.

9. E. Guy Talbott, "The Relation between Theology and Sociology," *The Biblical World* 46, no. 3 (1915): 170.

10. Brewer, "Sociology and Theology Reconsidered."

11. Karel Dobbelaere, "From Religious Sociology to Sociology of Religion: Toward Globalisation?," *Journal for the Scientific Study of Religion* 39 (2000): 433–47.

12. Neil Ormerod, "*Sensus Fidei* and Sociology: How Do We Find the Normative in the Empirical?" in *Learning from All the Faithful: A Contemporary Theology of the* Sensus Fidei, ed. Bradford Hinze and Peter Phan (Eugene, OR: Pickwick Publications, 2016), 89–102.

13. James Sweeney, "Theology and Sociology," in *Christianity and the Disciplines: The Transformation of the University*, ed. Oliver Crisp, Gavin D'Costa, Mervyn Davies, and Peter Hampson (London: T&T Clark, 2012), 105.

14. David Martin, *Reflections on Sociology and Theology* (Oxford, UK: Oxford University Press, 1997).

15. Andrew Greeley, "Sociology and Theology: Some Methodological Questions," *Proceedings of the Catholic Theological Society of America* 32 (2012): 32.

16. Flanagan, "The Return of Theology," 433.

17. David Martin, *On Secularization: Towards a Revised General Theory* (Aldershot, UK: Ashgate, 2007).

18. Jeff Wheeldon, "Theology as Sociology, Sociology as Theology," *Journal of Sociology and Christianity* 6, no. 2 (2016): 18.

19. Pilario, "Interdisciplinary Perspectives," 35.

20. Brewer, "Sociology and Theology."

21. Marcus Moberg and Tuomas Martikainen, "Religious Change in Market and Consumer Society: The Current State of the Field and New Ways Forward," *Religion* 48, no. 3 (2018): 418–35; Jayeel Cornelio, François Gauthier, Tuomas Martikainen, and Linda Woodhead, eds., *The Routledge International Handbook of Religion in Global Society* (London: Routledge, 2020).

22. Cornelio, "Popular Religion," 471.

23. Linda Woodhead, Hiroko Kawanami, and Christopher H. Partridge, eds., *Religions in the Modern World: Traditions and Transformations*, 2nd ed. (London: Routledge, 2009).

24. Kieran Flanagan, *Seen and Unseen: Visual Culture, Sociology and Theology* (New York: Palgrave Macmillan, 2004), 3.

25. Kieran Flanagan, "Sociology into Theology: The Unacceptable Leap," *Theory, Culture & Society* 25, nos. 7/8 (2008): 258.

26. Flanagan, "The Return of Theology," 440.

27. Martin, *Reflections*, 16.

28. Inja Inders and Matthew Robinson, eds., *What Does Theology Do, Actually?: Observing Theology and the Transcultural* (Leipzig, Germany: EVA, 2020).

29. Andrew Whitehead, Samuel Perry, and Joseph Baker, "Make America Christian Again: Christian Nationalism and Voting for Donald Trump in the 2016 Presidential Election," *Sociology of Religion* 79, no. 2 (2018): 147–71.

30. Jayeel Cornelio, "Claiming the Nation: Theological Nationalism in the Philippines," in Inders and Robinson, eds., *What Does Theology Do, Actually?*, 149–65.

31. Robert Cortegiano, "The Use of Sociology in the Study of the *Sensus Fidelium*: An Evaluation of the Contribution of Jerome Baggett," in Hinze and Phan, eds., *Learning from All the Faithful*, 120.

32. Pilario, "Interdisciplinary Perspectives."

33. Christian Smith, *The Sacred Project of American Sociology* (Oxford, UK: Oxford University Press, 2014).

34. Smith, *The Sacred Project*, 7–8.

35. Wheeldon, "Theology as Sociology."

36. Wheeldon, "Theology as Sociology."

37. Zygmunt Bauman, *Globalization: The Human Consequences* (Cambridge, UK: Polity Press, 1998); Zygmunt Bauman, *Liquid Love: On the Frailty of Human Bonds* (Cambridge, UK: Polity Press, 2003).

38. Sweeney, "Theology and Sociology," 114.

39. John Burkhard, "The *Sensus Fidelium*: Old Questions, New Challenges," in Hinze and Phan, eds., *Learning from All the Faithful*, 136.

40. Burkhard, "The *Sensus Fidelium*," 12.

41. Ormond Rush, "*Sensus Fidei*: Faith 'Making Sense' of Revelation," *Theological Studies* 62, no. 2 (2001): 255.

42. Gemma Tulud Cruz, "Theology as Conversation: *Sensus*

Fidelium and Doing Theology on/from Margins," in Hinze and Phan, eds., *Learning from All the Faithful*, 344–59.

43. Dorian Llywelyn, "Devotion, Theology and the *Sensus Fidelium*," *New Blackfriars* 98, no. 1074 (2017): 171–87.

44. Manuel Victor J. Sapitula, "Marian Piety and Modernity: The Perpetual Help Devotion as Popular Religion in the Philippines," *Philippine Studies: Historical & Ethnographic Viewpoints* 62, nos. 3/4 (2014): 399–424.

45. Peter J. Bräunlein, "'We Are 100% Catholic': Philippine Passion Rituals and Some Obstacles in the Study of Non-European Christianity," *Journal of Religion in Europe* 5, no. 3 (2012): 384–413, https://doi.org/10.1163/18748929-00503003; Cornelio, "Popular Religion."

46. Jerome Baggett, "Becoming Absence-Minded: Sociological Reflections on the *Sensus Fidelium*," *Proceedings of the Catholic Theological Society of America* 70 (2015).

47. Cruz, "Theology as Conversation," 350.

48. Cortegiano, "The Use of Sociology."

49. Llywelyn, "Devotion," 187.

50. Jayeel Cornelio, *Being Catholic in the Contemporary Philippines: Young People Reinterpreting Religion* (London: Routledge, 2016).

51. Cortegiano, "The Use of Sociology," 111.

52. Bryan Froehle, "Catholic Pastoral Sociology in the United States since Vatican II: Making a Path by Walking," *U.S. Catholic Historian* 25, no. 4 (2007): 85.

53. Michael Northcott, "Pastoral Theology and Sociology," in *The Blackwell Reader in Pastoral and Practical Theology*, ed. James Woodward and Stephen Pattison (Oxford, UK: Blackwell, 2000), 151–63.

54. Chris Dols and Herman Paul, "Introduction: Pastoral Sociology in Western Europe, 1940–1970," *Journal of Religion in Europe* 9, nos. 2/3 (2016): 99–105.

55. Second Vatican Council, *Christus Dominus* (Decree Concerning the Pastoral Office of Bishops in the Church), October 28, 1965, https://www.vatican.va/archive/hist_councils/ii_vatican_council/documents/vat-ii_decree_19651028_christus-dominus_en.html.

56. Froehle, "Catholic Pastoral Sociology."

57. Benjamin Ziemann, "The Practical Sociologist: Role and Performance of Pastoral Sociologists in the West German Catholic Church, 1945–1970," *Journal of Religion in Europe* 9, nos. 2/3 (2016): 133–56.

58. Susan Dunlap, "Culture-Coded Care: Ecclesial Beliefs, Practices, and Artifacts in Response to Illness," in *Pastoral Bearings: Lived Religion and Pastoral Theology*, ed. Jane Maynard, Leonard Hummel, and Mary Clark Moschella (Lanham, MD: Lexington Books), 76.

59. Ines Jindra and Michael Jindra, "How Do People Change their Lives? The Role of the Narrative Interview and the Biographical Trajectory for Social Work and Pastoral Care in the United States," *Pastoral Psychology* 68 (2019): 195–208.

60. Dunlap, "Culture-Coded Care."

61. Dunlap, "Culture-Coded Care," 75.

62. Esther Acolatse, "Pastoral Care and Counseling in Independent Evangelical Charismatic Churches in Ghana: A Barthian Theological Perspective," in Maynard et al., eds., *Pastoral Bearings*, 235–50.

63. Manuel Vasquez, "Structural Obstacles to Grassroots Pastoral Practice: The Case of a Base Community in Urban Brazil," *Sociology of Religion* 58, no. 1 (1997): 65.

64. Northcott, "Pastoral Theology."

65. Ziemann, "The Practical Sociologist," 153.

66. Sebastian Kim, *Theology in the Public Sphere: Public Theology as a Catalyst for Open Debate* (London: SCM Press, 2011).

67. Bonnie Miller-McLemore, "Pastoral Theology and Public Theology: Developments in the US," in *Pathways to the Public Square: Practical Theology in an Age of Pluralism*, ed. Elaine Graham and Anna Rowlands (Münster, Germany: LIT Verlag, 2005), 95–106.

68. Christine Schliesser, "Theology and Public Democratic Institutions: Public Theology in the Context of the German and Swiss National Ethics Councils," in *Religion and Democracy: Studies in Public Theology*, ed. Torsten Meireis and Rolf Schieder (Baden-Baden, Germany: Nomos, 2017), 155–70.

69. Clemens Wustmans, "Plain Language as Empowerment beyond a Faithful Middle-Class Public: Contributions of Public Theology to the Capability Approach of Social Justice," in Meireis and Schieder, eds., *Religion and Democracy*, 143–54.

70. Katie Day and Sebastian Kim, "State, Democracy and Community Organizing," in *A Companion to Public Theology*, ed. Sebastian Kim and Katie Day (Leiden, Netherlands: Brill, 2017), 105.

71. Torsten Meireis and Rolf Schieder, "Introduction: Democracy, Religion and Public Theology," in Meireis and Schieder, eds., *Religion and Democracy*, 9–18.

72. Vasquez, "Structural Obstacles."

73. James Farwell, "Liturgy and Public Theology," *Anglican Theological Review* 102, no. 2 (2020): 219–29.

74. William Holden, "Post Modern Public Administration in the Land of Promise: The Basic Ecclesial Community Movement of Mindanao," *Worldviews: Global Religions, Culture, and Ecology* 13, no. 2 (2019): 180–218.

75. Moberg and Martikainen, "Religious Change."

76. Kim, *Theology*, 3.

77. Jean-Guy Nadeau, "Public Theology in Pop Culture: Critical Uses and Functions of the Bible in Rock Music and Metal," in *Pathways to the Public Square: Practical Theology in an Age of Pluralism*, ed. Elaine Graham and Anna Rowlands (Münster, Germany: LIT Verlag, 2005), 157.

78. Meredith B. McGuire, *Lived Religion: Faith and Practice in Everyday Life* (Oxford, UK: Oxford University Press, 2008).

79. Inders and Robinson, *What Does Theology*.

80. Meireis and Schieder, "Introduction," 9 (see n. 71 above).

81. Jayeel Cornelio and Erron Medina, "Christianity and Duterte's War on Drugs in the Philippines," *Politics, Religion & Ideology* 20, no. 2 (2019): 151–69; Jayeel Cornelio, "The Philippines," in *Christianity in East and South-East Asia*, ed. Kenneth Ross, Todd Johnson, and Francis Alvarez, Edinburgh Companions to Global Christianity (Edinburgh, Scotland: Edinburgh University Press, 2020); Jayeel Cornelio and Ia Marañon, "A 'Righteous Intervention': Megachurch Christianity and Duterte's War on Drugs in the Philippines," *International Journal of Asian Christianity* 2, no. 2 (2019): 211–30.

82. Emmanuel S. De Guzman, "The Scent of Marginality: Odorizing the Difference in Migration Relations," in *Intercultural Church: Bridge of Solidarity in the Migration Context*, ed. Agnes M. Brazal and Emmanuel S. De Guzman (Alameda, CA: Borderless Press, 2015).

9. From Smelling like Sheep to Journeying Together

1. For example, see Dorian Llywelyn, "Devotion, Theology and the *Sensus Fidelium*," *New Blackfriars* 98, no. 1074 (2017): 171–87.

2. John Burkhard, "The *Sensus Fidelium*: Old Questions, New Challenges," in *Learning from All the Faithful: A Contemporary Theology of the* Sensus Fidei, ed. Bradford Hinze and Peter Phan (Eugene, OR: Pickwick Publications. 2016), 136.

3. Burkhard, "*Sensus Fidelium*," 12.

4. Ormond Rush, "*Sensus Fidei*: Faith 'Making Sense' of Revelation," *Theological Studies* 62, no. 2 (2001): 255.

5. Peter J. Bräunlein, "'We Are 100% Catholic': Philippine Passion Rituals and Some Obstacles in the Study of Non-European Christianity," *Journal of Religion in Europe* 5, no. 3 (2012): 384–413, https://doi.org/10.1163/18748929-00503003; Jayeel Cornelio, "Popular Religion and the Turn to Everyday Authenticity: Reflections on the Contemporary Study of Philippine Catholicism," *Philippine Studies: Historical and Ethnographic Viewpoints* 62, no. 3 (2014): 471–500.

6. Manuel Victor J. Sapitula, "Marian Piety and Modernity: The Perpetual Help Devotion as Popular Religion in the Philippines," *Philippine Studies: Historical & Ethnographic Viewpoints* 62, nos. 3/4 (2014): 399–424.

7. Gemma Tulud Cruz, "Theology as Conversation: *Sensus Fidelium* and Doing Theology on/from Margins," in *Learning from All the Faithful: A Contemporary Theology of the* Sensus Fidei, ed. Bradford Hinze and Peter Phan (Eugene, OR: Pickwick Publications, 2016), 350.

8. Llywelyn, "Devotion, Theology and the *Sensus Fidelium*,"187.

9. International Theological Commission, "Synodality in the Life and the Mission of the Church," March 2, 2018, nos. 11–41, https://www.vatican.va/roman_curia/congregations/cfaith/cti_documents/rc_cti_20180302_sinodalita_en.htm.

10. Massimo Faggioli, "From Collegiality to Synodality: Promise and Limits of Francis's 'Listening Primacy,'" *Irish Theological Quarterly* 85, no. 4 (2020): 352–69.

11. Amanda Osheim, "Stepping toward a Synodal Church," *Theological Studies* 80, no. 2 (2019): 373.

12. Osheim, "Stepping," 374.

13. Francis, "Address during the Ceremony Commemorating the Fiftieth Anniversary of the Institution of the Synod of Bishops," October 17, 2015, https://www.vatican.va/content/francesco/en/speeches/2015/october/documents/papa-francesco_20151017_50-anniversario-sinodo.html.

14. Francis, "Address during the Ceremony Commemorating the Fiftieth Anniversary."

15. Osheim, "Stepping," 378.

16. Osheim, "Stepping," 391.

17. See also "Synodality in the Life and Mission of the Church," no. 3.

18. Faggioli, "From Collegiality to Synodality," 366.

19. Faggioli, "From Collegiality to Synodality," 367–68.

20. Osheim, "Stepping," 370.

21. Pope Francis, "Address during the Ceremony Commemorating the Fiftieth Anniversary."

Index

A Discerning Church

POPE FRANCIS, LONERGAN, AND A THEOLOGICAL METHOD FOR THE FUTURE

Gerard Whelan, SJ

A Discerning Church presents a theological model for these changing times. It examines the thought of Bernard Lonergan and offers an assessment of the significance of Pope Francis and the church since the Second Vatican Council. It then explores major insights and issues, such as ecclesial reform, globalization, and sexuality, that will impact the future of the church.

978-0-8091-5446-3 Paperback 256 pages $29.95